Martina Maria Sam

The Challenge
of Spiritual Language

Rudolf Steiner's Linguistic Style

Translated by Marguerite A. Miller
and Douglas E. Miller

RUDOLF STEINER PRESS

Rudolf Steiner Press
Hillside House, The Square
Forest Row, East Sussex RH18 5ES

www.rudolfsteinerpress.com

Published by Rudolf Steiner Press in 2020

Originally published as *The Struggle for a New Language* in 2004 and reprinted under the title *The Challenge of Spiritual Language* in 2007 by Verlag am Goetheanum, Dornach, Switzerland

© Verlag am Goetheanum 2007
This edition © Rudolf Steiner Press 2020

A catalogue record for this book is available from the British Library

ISBN 978 1 85584 577 0

Cover by Andrew Morgan Design
Typeset by Höpcke, Hamburg, Germany
Printed and bound by 4Edge Ltd., Essex

Table of Contents

Preface

The seven essays that comprise this little book originated in the summer of 2003 as a first attempt at presenting my long-standing research into Rudolf Steiner's language and style. I have observed the increasing difficulty people—often academically educated people, in particular—have with this style, and have noted that more and more people find it laborious, complicated, and unscientific. These essays are, on the one hand, intended to make clear that Rudolf Steiner deliberately strove for another style and why he did so; and, on the other hand, to arouse the courage and interest necessary for others to make their own voyage of discovery into this special linguistic cosmos.

In the attempt to produce a representative, concentrated, and comprehensive description of this extensive material, a logical division into seven, self-contained essays became apparent. What was most important for me in this was to point out Rudolf Steiner's intentions in his specific and often original (linguistic) forms and, consequently, to create the introductory basis for a deeper understanding.

The first chapter introduces, by way of example, the comments of a few individuals—some of them prominent figures—who found Rudolf Steiner's style "grating;" these were people who were unable to muster any understanding at all for why he had to develop such an unconventional language. The main reasons for this style are rooted in the difficulties created by the need to report the results of spiritual research in a modern language entirely directed toward the material-sensory world. These reasons will be presented in a second chapter. Following a look at the specific character of Rudolf Steiner's lectures (chapter 3), two comprehensive stylistic principles are presented that permeate his entire body of work: characterization (chapter 4), and his special handling of the pictorial element in language (chapter 5). An entire essay is devoted to the creation of meditative verses and mantras (chapter 6). And in the final essay, a view is offered of the development of an artistic, linguistically creative element of spiritual scientific presentation that will only be possible in the future.

Of course, what is presented here can only be a first step. Many other approaches are yet to be developed, further discoveries to be made. From the many reactions and letters I received following the publication of these essays in *Das Goetheanum* during autumn, 2003, I was able to sense how many people were inspired to make further discoveries. This facilitated the notion of bringing the essays together once again and publishing them in book form for a wider audience.

Here I would like to offer my heartfelt thanks to Johannes Kiersch and Heinz Zimmermann who led me to this rich and fruitful field of research, and to my dear friends Marguerite and Douglas Miller who kindly translated these essays into English.

These essays first appeared in English in North America serialized in the *Newsletter of the Literary Arts and Humanities Section*.

Martina Maria Sam

Introduction

Recently, the PISA Study, a study comparing the reading ability of 15 year-old students around the world, has caused quite a sensation. The results of this study reflected a shocking picture of a growing lack of interest in reading and an inability to read. Around a third of the young people worldwide never read a book voluntarily. And for a significant number of students, even the simplest texts remain incomprehensible. There are many studies that point out that adults today are not much better off in regard to their ability to read and to enjoy it. Fewer and fewer people pick up any books at all; many cannot understand what they (have to) read; and even the length of time spent with each book is growing ever shorter.

In the face of these general tendencies, it is not at all surprising that people interested in anthroposophy increasingly say that reading Rudolf Steiner's works is too difficult for them. There are demands that his awkward, unnecessarily complicated, and "old fashioned" style be recast in "modern German." The content, according to those who make these arguments, is so worthy and inspiring that it should not remain unknown to a modern audience. They argue that, in order for those seeking this content to find entry to it, it makes sense to free it from its old-fashioned form.

Those who make such demands are following a trend of the times: "Reading," in the sense of the PISA study, is understood purely as an information gathering process. It is a matter of extracting content statements—whether from a text, from tables, organizational charts, or graphs, is of no real consequence—and integrating them into a pre-existing body of knowledge. According to the authors of the study, "Reading literacy is understanding, using, and reflecting on written texts, in order to achieve one's goals, to develop one's knowledge and potential, and to participate in society."[1]

This kind of "reading" is strongly favored by modern media, especially the internet. According to the literacy researcher Goedart Palm, "The net-oriented reader 'scans' texts, searches out chunks of text instead of reading-intensive texts."[2] People jump from one piece of information to another, from sensation to sensation. This means, however, that they are really no longer connecting with the text, or not allowing themselves to enter into it more deeply. In the face of the enormous flood of information that meets us today, it is understandable that such a reading style is valued and practiced. How else could we cope with the massive volume of material? And how else could we find in it what is relevant for us?

And yet we might ask the provocative question: Doesn't this method of teaching reading promote a sense of reading overload, and an increasing inability to read? How am I to be filled with enthusiasm for the process of reading, for the structure and the specific language of texts, when they are there merely to convey *bits of information* to me which I could acquire much more quickly through other means and media—charts, tables, films, pictures, and so forth?

We might ask ourselves what actually draws us to books that we read over and over, that continually excite us and uplift us, even though we already "know" them—

at least their content. There are books that we read again and again because in and from them we discover something new and different with every reading, because we are changed by them.—What is the secret of these books?

This cannot be summarized in a few words. Such books are multilayered and multifaceted, unfathomable; they are inexhaustible. Their meaning is not found only in what can be drawn from them as information or intellectual knowledge. What inspires, what is multilayered about them, is drawn from the interplay of form and content. Not only *what* is said in them, but *how* it is said—the composition, the dynamic of the motifs, the linguistic methodology, the stylistic levels, the inner drama, etc.— all this is more essential to, is truly a more intrinsic part of, the whole.

A part of the "mystery" of good books lies in awakening sensitivity and feeling without falling into formal intellectual analysis. This is important for reading education in the schools as well as for our own reading. Schooling our attention as preparation for entering into a text, for the kinds of images it uses, for the shaping of thoughts, its musicality or plasticity, the scope of the words and tonal qualities of the language, and much more, in short, to grasp a text as a "work of art," to learn to love it—these can open doorways to another, deeper reading.

This kind of deeper reading is indispensable if we are to read Rudolf Steiner's works in an appropriate and modern way. His books and also his lectures—taking into account all of the imperfections in the way they have been handed down to us—are in a certain sense works of art, a unity of content and form (see chapter 7). What he related from his spiritual research appears first of all *in* and *with* language. What is essential cannot be experienced at all, cannot be communicated at all, if the merely objective information is separated from the linguistic presentation. As Rudolf Steiner wrote generally about anthroposophical books in his autobiography, *Mein Lebensgang* [The course of my life].

"... a properly written anthroposophical book should be an awakener of the spiritual life in the reader, not a collection of information. Reading it should not merely be reading, it should be an experience with inner jolts, tensions, and releases."[3] This is the clear intention he always had for his own works.

The path here is the goal: the study of spiritual scientific works, the effort to understand them, the inner activity it takes to penetrate to their spirit—these things are the essential elements of what happens as we read. "When someone reads an anthroposophical book, he must enter into it with his whole being."[4] The reader must, once again, experience reading a book a little as it was in the Middle Ages when "reading a book was ... something like growth; productive forces were set loose within the human organism."[5]

In this sense, it is appropriate when reading Rudolf Steiner to practice a completely different kind of reading, one that has been lost to many contemporary readers. We can, as a result of such a practice, become aware of many stylistic methods and linguistic peculiarities that allow us not only to penetrate deeper into the spirit of what is said but also deeper into the spirit of language itself. If we approach Rudolf Steiner's style in this way, if we penetrate the character and intention of his linguistic forms, we get beyond the mere level of meaning in language.

Participating in the form gestures of language and their echo in us leads to a loftier level, to an imaginatively creative level of language from which our own linguistic capacity and style can be enlivened and enriched anew.

"If only it were all said more succinctly!"

Is Rudolf Steiner's Language
Still Understandable Today?

In autumn 2001 *Rudolf Steiner's Occult Science, An Outline* appeared in print in "modern German." The new version of *Occult Science* was written—it would perhaps be better to say that it was translated—by Edith Attinger, a Swiss Waldorf parent. In the introduction she sets forth what moved her to do this: she wanted to "make this significant work available to a wider audience through [her] modernized version" so that "Rudolf Steiner's insights and knowledge, which are still valid today, can continue to promote a true understanding of the evolution of humanity and our planet."[6]

She relates what she experienced as she was reading: She had "some difficulty … following Rudolf Steiner's peculiar and somewhat outdated way with language." She felt simultaneously "drawn by Steiner's deep knowledge …, but somewhat helpless in the face of his linguistic peculiarity." Therefore, she began—"at first mildly annoyed as [she] sought to come to a real understanding of Steiner, and then with increasing enthusiasm and devotion—'to translate' his multilayered text sentence by sentence into a German that is much easier for us as modern readers to understand."

Edith Attinger's statements are symptomatic of an opinion held by many people today who are interested in the knowledge of Rudolf Steiner but who feel put off by his language. They want new editions of his books in which the 'essence,' as it were, the most important statements, would be reproduced in a shortened and linguistically modernized form. They want the content but not the form, not the clothing, which is experienced as outdated or not entirely successful.

The Irritation with Rudolf Steiner's Style

A professor I respect greatly and with whom I have conducted long and interesting conversations about anthroposophy summed it up this way: "You know, I have tried again and again to read Steiner, but my philosophical education always stood in the way." From subsequent statements he made I gathered that what he intended to say is that "Someone who has as much education in philosophy as I have finds no clarity in this conceptually diffuse language."

In a widely noted guest column in the newspaper *Die Drei* (Number 2/2002), the Hamburg journalist Wolfgang Müller-El Abd set forth why, according to him, anthroposophy is not really scientific. Without going explicitly into Steiner's linguistic style, he describes some experiences while reading Steiner's works, for example *Occult Science*. "Do we learn here about *Steiner's* world or the *world*? Basically it is a long series of presentations and reports, sometimes illustrated by comparisons, sometimes quite abrupt, in any case without stringent, argumentative derivation."[7] It should be "maintained that a *scientific* presentation must offer other forms of provability." "Thus we see before us an impressive spiritual panorama—but no scientific description." Referring to the book *Mysticism at the Dawn of Modern Spiritual Life* he claims, "Basically there are lectures about Steiner, Steiner, and more Steiner."[8] Reading the transcripts of the lectures, he notes a "very nearly infinite distance between the knowing teacher and the amazed listener."[9] Finally, he makes one more noteworthy statement in his essay about which literary form he would find more satisfactory to convey Steiner's message: "It would mean a lot if these perspectives were first made available to us in another way—as something like a poetic text. In the meantime, things become quite troublesome where conceptual demands are made."[10]

In a reply to Müller-El Abd's presentation, the psychoanalyst Peter Petersen states his own reasons for what is to him Steiner's oftentimes "unbearable language": On the one hand, there is its imprisonment in *Art Nouveau*—the fact it is time bound; and on the other hand the problem lies in the fact that "it tries to be poetic and yet is situated far from what is considered poetry today."[11]

In the art historian Beat Wyss' 1996 book *The Will to Art*—in which there is a chapter entitled 'The Goetheanum, Metamorphoses of a Poem"—he makes the following assertions about Rudolf Steiner's language: "Steiner's written lectures lack the life of charismatic speech; the words lie on the page like dead leaves, windblown across our path. The message behind the stilted redundance of the sentences is deciphered by the uninitiated reader with great difficulty. Steiner's language remains evocation; its task is to summon the truth, only to vanish in the light cast when truth appears."[12]

These examples of recent statements about Steiner's

language summarize symptomatically the points that cause many modern readers discomfort. His style is experienced as unique to him and old-fashioned, as conceptually unclear, too stilted or redundant, too ambiguous. And then there is another quality that is more difficult to grasp: There is something poetic about the language—which is otherwise unknown in texts with scientific intent—although it is not designated as "poetic language."

If we turn our attention to how Steiner's contemporaries experienced his style, we encounter similar statements. Paul Klee—whose wife Lili was deeply engaged with anthroposophy according to reports by their son Felix Klee—writes in his diary entry of October 10, 1918 that he was reading "in the book by Steiner" [probably *Theosophy*]. And he complains, "If only it were all said more succinctly! In ten pages. To me, people who write whole books are more and more puzzling."[13] And four days later he writes, "Theosophy? I became especially suspicious about the appearance of color he described there…. This is working with suggestion. The truth, however, does not require the absence of resistance in order to come to the fore. Of course, I have only read portions of the book because its banalities soon made it unenjoyable."[14]

In 1898, Rainer Maria Rilke corresponded with Rudolf Steiner in his (Steiner's) capacity as the editor of the *Magazin für Literatur*, and dedicated a copy of his drama *Without Presence* to him. In 1926, Rilke writes to the editor Hans Reinhart how much he regrets that Reinhart had begun the first issue of the magazine *Individualität* [Individuality] with a reprint of a Steiner lecture (*The Psychology of the Arts*, GA 271). "I expect that I am not the only one to regret that you decided to begin this publication with these remarks by Rudolf Steiner which were more or less taken from a lecture and left in a very miserable and unsatisfactory state—far beyond any linguistic form."[15]

In February, 1919, Hermann Hesse signed Rudolf Steiner's appeal "To the German People and the Cultured World" after he had heard the lecture on February 5, 1919, and which had made a "very good, convincing impression"[16] on him. In 1944, however, he states in a letter to an unknown recipient, "I knew Dr. Steiner only in passing and often sought in vain to read some of his books. They remained absolutely intolerable, if only because of their dreadfully bloodless language."[17]

What a bouquet of the most varied reproaches and objections! For one of them, Rudolf Steiner's language is too bloodless; for another, it is too subjective; a third finds only banalities in his books; while the next person emphasizes the unique quality of his language; and still another experiences it as evocation through which the truth is to be summoned.

Counterexamples can also be found. There are contemporary reviews of Steiner's books that emphasize the clarity of his language. In 1911, Max Brod wrote, "His language is by far clearer and calmer than Blavatsky's, somewhat wide-ranging but structured logically, essentially irrefutable. ... he works in a scientific way rather than one of faith."[18] Then there is Julius Frisch, who wrote in a review of *Welt- und Lebensanschauungen im 19. Jahrhundert* [Views on the world and life in the 19th century], "The language of the work is easily grasped. There are no pedantic, lengthy expressions to disturb the reader's enjoyment. The presentation is in every respect masterly and original."[19] Even today there is a host of people who are especially moved by Steiner's style.

However, this was the place to let a group of personalities speak in a symptomatic way—all of whom had a certain personal connection to anthroposophy and/or Rudolf Steiner, and all of whom were irritated in various ways by how Steiner put his researches into words. For these irritations make clear that Rudolf Steiner apparently cultivated a special, unusual kind of language.

Seeking a New Language

What moved Rudolf Steiner to develop such an individual, "peculiar" style? More precisely, what constitutes his "peculiarities"? And what are the effects of these unusual linguistic structures and stylistic peculiarities?

Rudolf Steiner himself spoke countless times—often in a way that was a bit veiled—about his style which was necessary for anthroposophical spiritual science. It becomes quite clear in his remarks that he chose and formed his lecture and writing style in full consciousness, and that this is in no way the result of an inadequate mastery of the language, conditions of the time, or an old-fashioned Austrian dialect.[20] He also fully realized that with this style, he did not fit into the academic context of his time. This is shown in the following citation from Steiner's lectures to the workers that simultaneously sheds light on *why* he had to find a new kind of language to present the results of his spiritual scientific research:

"If someone now wants to come to anthroposophy, I

would have to say that he must relearn the language in a completely new way. For you will see that when some modern scholars lecture about something—wow!—it's like it comes out of a machine. It is different than when someone lectures out of spiritual science, out of anthroposophy. Then we must continually look for the words; we must inwardly take up the words in a way that is always new. And afterwards—when we have formed the words—it is only then that we become truly concerned that they did not actually describe the right thing. With anthroposophy there is a completely different relationship to those who are listening than there is with modern day scholars. Modern scholars no longer worry about language. In anthroposophy, one must always worry about language.—You see, that is what comes to light in a peculiar way when I write my books; then I am in a constant, I would say inner unrest about forming the language correctly so that people can also understand what is being written. What must be created there with language is something new. Modern educated people simply say that I write in a poor style, that I do not write in proper German, because they are accustomed to putting the words in a certain order, one after the other, like clockwork. They do not speak from the soul. Therefore they are unaccustomed to someone forming his sentences differently than they do."[21]

"A constant struggle for an expression that seems sufficient ..."

Why Rudolf Steiner Had to Develop a New Language

In one of her "Frankfurt Lectures on Poetics" the poet Ingeborg Bachmann expresses sensitively the relationship between language and reality which, at the same time, characterizes the relationship between language and knowledge: "Reality will always be met with a new language where a moral, cognitional jolt occurs—not where an attempt is made to make language new per se, as though language itself could drive home some knowledge and reveal to us some experience, neither of which we ever had. When language is only tinkered with so that it feels like new, it soon takes revenge and exposes the intent. A new language must have a new way of moving, and it only has this new gait when a new spirit inhabits it."[22]

Around 1920, Rudolf Steiner already pointed out how contemporary language is often used so that "theories"—perception by way of language, by way of a certain use of language—arise as though by themselves. "But since language—every modern, civilized language—has gradually created phrases, maxims, even whole theories that now exist in the language, we only need to change slightly what is already in the language in order to appear to have a creation of our own making. However, we have basically done just a little rearranging of what was already there."[23]

Ingeborg Bachmann and Rudolf Steiner are speaking about the same phenomenon. Through the history of civilization, through the inflationary use of language in the past 150 years, and through the increasing concentration on the physical-material world, rigid circles of meaning have become ensconced around individual words. On the one hand, these circles of meaning not only suggest certain connections between words, but seem to produce them automatically; on the other hand, they make it increasingly impossible to penetrate to the most intimate content of the words, to their sources, to the original gestures of the word and its meaning.

Just as an impenetrable thicket of thorns grew around the sleeping princess in the fairy tale of Sleeping Beauty—its branches woven tightly together so that it was almost impossible to reach the beauty resting in the middle—so it is with the sleeping princess that is the word. If we—to use Bachmann's words —only "tinker with" language, we become stuck in the thorns; we become the prisoners of the thickets surrounding the word. But where a "moral, cognitional jolt" occurs, a new language will also arise. The thorny thicket of language does not yield as easily as it does to the prince in the fairy tale; but those who do not shy away from difficulties and scratches will be able to wake the sleeping princess of language. And for every "prince," for every word awakener, it will look different; it will reveal a different face.

The Battle with Language

If we now put ourselves in Rudolf Steiner's position when the Anthroposophical Society was founded, we can easily imagine the difficult situation in which he found himself as he sought a suitable way to describe spiritual content. In a time when poets and writers first spoke about a language crisis, when they experienced the language as "flaccid and worthless from overuse"[24]—during the first widespread blossoming of materialism in society—Rudolf Steiner was to speak to people about the spiritual world, about spheres of a completely different kind than those of the familiar, sensory world of daily life. And he could only make use of the language he had at hand, with all the restrictions and difficulties that came with it.

Rudolf Steiner often spoke about these problems with language and communication. In particular, he spoke of them in his basic works which were consciously placed in the public arena. Thus we find in *Occult Science, An Outline*: "Nevertheless it became noticeable to the author in a number of places how brittle the descriptive means available to him prove to be compared to what is revealed by supersensible research ... Experiences concerning such things deviate so greatly from the experiences of the sensory realms that presenting them necessarily creates a constant struggle for an expression that seems in any way sufficient. Anyone willing to examine in detail this attempt at description will note perhaps that an effort has been made through the method of presentation to provide much of what is impossible for the dry word to convey."[25] "To name the loftier things of existence, we must still employ the words of common language. And these words express only what is sensory for sensory observation."[26] In another place he writes, "The words of our language all too easily call forth imaginations that are taken from life in the present time ... our language is calibrated to the sensory world. And what we describe with it immediately takes on the character of this sensory world."[27]

In his essay *Language and the Spirit of Language*,[28] Rudolf Steiner describes in detail the difficulties met by someone who wants to communicate the "inner experience of a spiritual reality." "If he now wants to make reports of his observations, his battle with the language begins. He seeks to use everything possible within the realm of language in order to create an image of what he observes. He searches everywhere in the realm of what is linguistically possible, from similar sounds to turns of phrase." If we do our best in this way, "the battle can find the best, the most beautiful outcome. A moment arrives when it is felt that the spirit of the language takes up what is observed. The words and phrases arrived at take on an element of spirituality; they cease to 'mean' what they usually mean and slip into what is observed.—It is at that point that a kind of lively intercourse with the spirit of the language begins. Language takes on a personal quality; we come to terms with it as though it were another person."[29]

Impetus for a Free Spiritual Collaboration

It becomes clear through this description that the spiritual researcher has to create a different relationship to language than the usual one which only considers content. He has to overcome language's pure "element of meaning", the concepts that are closely bound to the words: "The seer thinks without words and is then compelled to pour what is experienced without words into already fully-formed language ... He can communicate because of the fact that he strips away what is conceptual in the language. This is why it so significant for us to understand *that it is more important how the seer says something than what he says*."[30]

Many passages could be cited where Rudolf Steiner speaks about this central principle of style, that the how of the spiritual researcher's language is more important than the what, the mere content. The how of the language—the whole way it is formed: the sounds, rhythms, images, syntax, composition, and more.[31]—But what does this other forming of the language demand of the reader? What must he be prepared for while he reads?

Rudolf Steiner often stresses that a definite inner attitude is demanded if one wants to take up supersensible perceptions. "Bringing forth something of a spiritual scientific nature means inviting the person to collaborate in his soul. People today do not want to do that. All spiritual science must be an invitation to such inner activity, which means that it must lead every observation to a place where there are no longer any points of reference in outer-sensory observation and the inner play of forces moves freely."[32] And early on, in 1907, he states: "A spiritual scientific book cannot be read in the same way that other books are read. It must be written so that it calls forth one's own activity. The more the reader has to struggle with it, the more that lies between the lines, the healthier it is."[33]

Thus, because of the particular nature of what Rudolf Steiner wanted to depict—the character and facts of spiritual realities—he was obliged to deal with the language differently than is usually the case. In this process, he had to take something else into consideration: Finding ways of describing things so that there was nothing subliminal in the information and nothing that could limit the freedom of the listener or reader. He wanted to "bring forth facts" of the sensory, the historical, and the supersensible world, but to arrange the presentation of these facts so that "based on these facts, the listener or reader is in a position to form his own judgment because the author or lecturer was renouncing having even the slightest influence on this judgment."[34]

The realm of freedom is protected by the individual's own strong inner activity—an activity required when reading spiritual scientific works in this way: What someone wants to build up inwardly on his own cannot overpower him subliminally; what someone wants to judge for himself must first be penetrated by his own inner activity.

Uncovering the Inner Gestures of Language

From this, we can also understand Rudolf Steiner's negative response to the continuous demands made on him to offer his works in a more "popular" style. "I have always struggled against this because it is essentially a part of how they should be—that they are not popular. If what is offered in our spiritual scientific literature is poured into all kinds of blurry forms…and this is then brought before the public, on the one hand only ease will be served, and on the other hand, they will do mischief. Because mischief will always arise when an attempt is made to behold the spirit in an easy, thoughtless way. The work we carry out when we learn to understand a more difficult text is an inner training; it is something that contributes to our forming a relationship to the spiritual world in the right way.

Thus it is a part—or should be a part—of the essential character of our literature that you really think in the most comprehensive way when you take up these things, that you transform your thoughts into activity; you should bring everything at your disposal from your previous knowledge, from your prior reading, into connection with what anthroposophical literature contains."[35]

The inner activation of the reader or listener, the unfolding of the individual's own inner activity, the impetus to take up the information with healthy human understanding and to unite it with existing world knowledge—these were what Rudolf Steiner thought were important in his method of presentation, in his style. Taking up spiritual scientific content should, in this sense, create capacities and stimulate a new perception that corresponds to this content. The tight connection between word and concept, between the form of the word and its meaning content, must be loosened, clearing away the thorny thicket of etymology—of what is merely about the concept—and letting us see once again the inner gesture of language. An essential quality of the spiritual can be experienced in what lies between the sounds, words, sentences—something the reader himself must build up actively. The form of the presentation is already a means of spiritual perception: "In order for us to come once again to a … living thinking, the means of expression in our language must once be re-enlivened."[36]

The way Rudolf Steiner tried concretely to re-enliven the means of expression in language will be shown with examples in the essays that follow.

"To turn and move the language so that its shortcomings are not experienced"

The Special Character of the Lectures

As a spiritual scientist, Rudolf Steiner faced the task of bringing the results of spiritual research into a sphere where it could be communicated. In the continuous revisions to the prefaces of his fundamental books, in many lectures, in the small essay, "Language and the Spirit of Language" (GA 36), Steiner describes the difficulties he had to wrestle with and the misunderstandings he had to clear up in the process. He also takes it up from another perspective when he says in one of his numerous notebooks, "And thus I experience deeply that I am now in a position to embody in human language what I have succeeded in researching in the spiritual world … only if I draw or set down a few strokes of the pen so that not only is the head engaged but the other organ systems as well … What is important here is that through these strokes of the pen, I give expression to thought and thus fix it. Thus there are wagonloads of my old notebooks that I never look at any more, because that is not why they exist. They exist so that what I brought with difficulty from the spirit can be brought to the point that it can be clothed in words so that it can gain access to memory."[37]

From these remarks we can gather what a difficult and laborious process it is to bring into words what is observed in the spirit—and thus to make it something that can be communicated. In order to achieve this in a way that does not pressure the reader or listener, that does not overpower him with fixed imaginations, emotions, and associations, but respects his inner freedom, Rudolf Steiner had to find his own individual and new ways of dealing with language.

The Audience Participates

Rudolf Steiner's collected works encompass two different textual elements: the transcripts of the lectures and the works that were written for publication.[38] What emerges clearly in the following words from Rudolf Steiner's autobiography, *Mein Lebensgang* [The course of my life] is that lecturing and writing were quite different things in his consciousness and technique: "There is actually in this duality of the private and the public writings something that stems from two different sources. The completely public writings are the result of what struggled and worked in me; in the private printings [the published manuscripts of the lectures that were intended only for members], the Society struggles and participates with me. I listen to what resonates in the soul life of the membership and, as I live within what I hear there, the methodology of the lectures arises."[39] And somewhat later he says, "What appears in the published writings is appropriate to the demands of anthroposophy as such; in the manner indicated, the soul constellation of the whole Society has participated in the way the private publications developed."[40]

It is clear from this that Rudolf Steiner was always attentive during his lectures to what he could "overhear" from the "soul needs" of his audience. He never held lectures that he had worked out for himself in the quiet of his study and then simply placed before his audience, but instead he spoke, to a great extent, *from out of his audience.* He took into account the local, historical, personal surroundings into which he spoke. The whole thrust of his lectures—in thought and language—is different depending on whether, for example, he conducts them in England or Germany, whether he spoke in 1906 or 1923, whether he offered a course for academics or was involved in a conversation with the workers at the Goetheanum.

In the second lecture of the so-called "Swiss Speaker's Course"[41] he also encouraged the budding lecturers "to develop a feel for the fact that something is not only correct but that it is justifiable in its context, that it can be good in a certain context and bad in another…. We must know how we may allow things in a certain context that in another context would not be permitted."[42]

To this end, for example, we can study the lectures that Rudolf Steiner held in Torquay during the summer of 1924 (*Das Initiatenbewußtsein* [Initiate consciousness], GA 243). We sense the way he encounters the character of the English folk through how direct and down-to-earth he is there, even with the loftiest occult things. Or we can look at the so-called *Arbeitervorträge* ([Lectures to the workers], GA 347–354). In these "conversations" with the construction workers building the Goetheanum, Rudolf Steiner uses a much stronger and more direct graphic quality and exhibits a completely different congeniality than in his other lectures.

This strong immersion in his audience is also partly responsible for the distinctive linguistic flow of the lectures—one that seems unusual to many readers—that is reflected in the sentence construction, in the many personal asides, the numerous repetitions, and so forth. However, what is especially irritating is the placement of the verb in the subordinate clauses (the verb is often found earlier in these clauses rather than in its grammatically correct placement at the end in German) and the complicated syntactic construction.

An example can make this clear (all the verbs that have been moved forward are set in italics): "Wenn nun auch Anthroposophie durchaus *ausgegangen ist*, von wissenschaftlichen Grundlagen,/ so musste sie sich,/ da sie eben mit den umfassenden,/ alle Menschen interessierenden großen Daseinsrätseln zu tun hat,/ so musste sie sich eben so entwickeln,/ dass sie *entgegenkommt* dem Verständnis auch des einfachsten Menschengemütes,/ dass sie *entgegenkommt* den praktischen Zeitbedürfnissen des menschlichen Seelen- und Geisteslebens,/ die da *suchen* inneren Halt für die Seele,/ Sicherheit für die Seele/ Kraft zum Handeln,/ Glauben an die Menscheit,/ an die menschliche Bestimmung."[43]

For a clearer impression, we can read this sentence aloud—first, as it stands, then so that the sentence is rendered in the usual way. Thus, for example at the end: "die da inneren Halt für die Seele, Sicherheit für die Seele, Kraft zum Handeln, Glauben an die Menschheit, an die menschliche Bestimmung *suchen*." When we now carefully observe what occurs through the shift, we note that the movement of the verb forward in the clause is a great help to the listener. He knows right at the beginning of the subordinate clause to what kind of movement he should attune his soul. To come back to the end of the clause: the striving inner gesture called forth by the verb *suchen* [to seek] is extended to all the more specific elements that follow it. On the other hand, if I am unaware of this inner direction from the beginning, I first have to listen additively, statically to the list of the various goals— and by the time I know what I should do (namely, *seek*), I have probably already forgotten the first attribute. Positioning the verb at the beginning, on the other hand, offers a kind of "animated keynote" for the whole, to which the soul can attune itself; as a result, the soul will hear the subsequent parts of the sentence in a different, "more prepared" way.

Another peculiarity that finds expression in the above example is its complicated syntax. There are so many subordinate clauses! How much patience is called for in order to read the sentence through to its end! To *read* it! If, on the other hand, we read the sentence aloud—thus making ourselves listeners as well—we soon notice how well we can inwardly follow along in spite of the complexity of the sentence structure. We even notice how wonderfully the sentence fits the rhythm of breathing and speaking. For this reason, I have inserted into the example a long-forgotten punctuation mark that later became our comma, the virgule [/]. It organizes the text according to the rhythm of speech, whereas our modern punctuation is based on grammatical sense.—The first printings of the Bible from the 15th and 16th centuries were still intended to be read aloud, thus with the listener in mind. In them we find again both of the striking principles in Rudolf Steiner's lectures: the forward placement of the verb in the subordinate clause and the division according to the rhythm of speech by using the virgule.[44]

As we became more and more a society that reads, we eventually lost this rhetorical way of writing; the typical way of printing text developed. Therefore, this rhetorical way of writing appears to us today as old-fashioned and complicated. But anyone who allows himself to enter into it without prejudice, and who genuinely tries to *hear through reading*, recognizes that this rhetorical style makes of listening a completely different process. It becomes a process that addresses not only the intellect by merely emphasizing the meaning, but breathing, through the rhythm of speech—thus the feeling human being—and also the realm of the will through the forward position of the verb.

A Continuous Element of Activity and Development

Rudolf Steiner used this medium very consciously; for him, a lecture was fundamentally different from an essay or a book.[45] Thus we can also understand why he often pointed out that he could not give lectures like his academic contemporaries: "He [the spiritual scientific researcher] cannot, for example, presume to say that a lecture he has given for the twelfth time would be easier to deliver because he has it firmly in his memory. In spiritual science—if one wants to be really honest—one cannot carry anything into his memory in this way, but instead must always express it anew as the result of inner soul work, not memory. Thus a lecture given for the fourteenth or fifteenth time is as new as the first time. It is a much more willed execution, a continuous element of activity, a continuous development of activity in the soul. Thus an honest, spiritual scientific representation which presents something based on a direct relationship with the spiritual world, will always attempt to coin the words anew."[46]

For this reason, Rudolf Steiner could not base his lectures on a carefully formulated written manuscript; his (lecture) preparation could only consist in "inner composure"[47]: "A person can also prepare himself but this preparation is a kind of practice ... What is needed as a basis for this production [the holding of a lecture] is composure, calm, so that the product can emerge from a quieted soul."[48]

Even the repetitions so many readers complain about are, in part, attributable to this structure of his lectures which is oriented towards listening. Most of us know very well the phenomenon of straying for a few seconds when listening—of being hung up on a provocative or otherwise touching thought—and losing the train of thought. How grateful we are for repetitions when that happens!

If we also take seriously the statement by Rudolf Steiner that "how a clairvoyant says something *is* more than what he says,"[49] then we must look at the principle of repetition from a different perspective. We will often find that repetition is only repetition at first glance; on second glance, we see that what was said was changed through fine nuances, that a new aspect is presented as a result, that what was apparently repeated has taken on a new color as a result of what was said in the mean time.

In a lecture in which Rudolf Steiner looks back on his futile attempts to write up his research on the subject of the senses,[50] he explains afterwards why it is more successful when done orally: He explains that in an oral lecture we have the possibility of "turning and moving the language, and making things understandable through repetitions, so that we do not so strongly feel the shortcomings in our language which is not yet adequate for such supersensible existence.[51]

In summary, we can say that there are two especially distinctive characteristics about Rudolf Steiner's lectures: they had to be taken hold of after intense inner composure and attunement to the moment and, in this sense, were a "momentary production out of the spirit;"[52] and in their linguistic formulation, they carry a rhetorical flow, a relationship to the listener that has been completely lost to us today and is therefore foreign to us. Nevertheless, deeper consideration will show that in their specific linguistic form, Rudolf Steiner's lectures were created just as consciously—in the sense of true spiritual knowledge—as his written works.

"… that we really feel each word to be inadequate"

Characterizing Rather Than Defining

It may be surprising at first that Rudolf Steiner often spoke of language in a way that can be described as "linguistically skeptical." Particularly in the lectures on the social question he points to how tragic it is that today people think in words rather than thoughts, that they are satisfied when they can affirm an object with a linguistic expression—then frequently do just the opposite by taking the word to be the thing. Used this way, language today becomes a hindrance rather than a help to drawing close to the spiritual world.

Emancipation from Nomenclature

In this sense, Rudolf Steiner again and again asks the audience of his lectures to "emancipate" themselves from language. By this, he means that they should not confuse the word with the thing, but should see words as mere gestures, indications, tokens by means of which we can arrive at the living (metalinguistic) concept. As a model for this inner attitude towards language, on more than one occasion Rudolf Steiner mentions proper names: Today no one would expect a "Mister Miller" to come through the door with a sack of flour over his shoulder; similarly with other words, we should avoid drawing conclusions about the character of something based on its name.

At first this seems to contradict all of the work Rudolf Steiner inaugurated in speech formation and eurythmy—where it is actually a matter of arriving at an experience of what is expressed through a feeling for the sounds of a word. When Rudolf Steiner says that human beings must emancipate themselves from language, he has another aspect of this in mind—the liberation from what he calls the purely lexicographic element of language, from constrained imaginations, from the "singular meanings" that have attached themselves to individual expressions during the last few centuries.

It is in this sense that we are to understand the etymological observations that Rudolf Steiner intersperses throughout his lectures. He wants to tear his audience away from the condensed meanings of words, meanings that automatically intrude with the sound of words; he wants to lead them back to the original—often wider—realm of the image in order to loosen the hardened idea carried by the word. For example: "grasp" does not just mean "getting it" or "understanding it;" but we should also have the visual sense of "grasping."[53] "Fairly" not only has the meaning of "somewhat", but is related to "to be fair."[54] "Right" not only refers to a collection of dusty laws; the word originally had the meaning of "righting," in the sense of "putting a situation right."[55] "Spellbinding" is not only a synonym for "charming" or "lovely"—the word "bind," in the sense of a strong restriction of movement, plays into it.[56]

According to Rudolf Steiner, our language in the present time is actually suited only to the physical world. The adequate phrase, the appropriate word no longer exist for the whole complexity of spiritual or psychological facts as they once did in times past.[57] How then, we ask ourselves, can we speak in any way correctly about spiritual matters today?

As in other fields, Goethe seems to have been a significant contributor to Rudolf Steiner's search for a language appropriate to the spirit. Rudolf Steiner emphasizes in many of his lectures that Goethe's capacity to set concepts and ideas in motion, as well as his introduction of mobile concepts into scientific life, were "something new" and his "central discovery."[58]

The magic formula that Rudolf Steiner used in connection with Goethe for his modern presentation of spiritual content was: characterization rather than definition. This sounds quite easy to begin with, but it has many levels and aspects that need to be taken into consideration.

At first, "characterization" means that we approach something by presenting it from various sides. Rudolf Steiner liked to bring the example of the tree that must be photographed from at least four sides if we are to create a somewhat appropriate idea of it. While definition eliminates everything that is accidental, everything that is concrete, in order to achieve a level of abstraction that includes every possibility imaginable, with characterization we are conscious that the content or concept we are trying to approach, to circumscribe, per se has something incomplete, something open about it. More aspects, more perspectives can be found that are as yet unknown—the concept that we have created can grow if the concept "is a living one": "Here the word is handled in such a way that each word is experienced as something inadequate, every phrase as something insufficient, and we have the urge to characterize from the most varied sides what we want to set forth before humanity—to a certain extent, even to move around the thing and to characterize it from the most varied sides. I have often emphasized that this must be anthroposophy's method of presentation."[59]

When characterizing in this way, we must try as much as possible to begin with concrete personal experiences. The audience (reader) must then put together the various images, the individual aspects—perhaps even supplement them with his own experiences—in order to create an open middle space, an emerging concept that is alive.

Anyone who has already read something by Rudolf Steiner knows the experiences connected with this method of characterization which, at first, leave many (particularly academically trained people) in despair about how to read the text. Instead of offering "clear" definitions (such as "an ether body is …") at the beginning a book, the concept of the ether body and phenomena connected with it, for example, are developed and described from always new and different aspects. Just compare the introduction of these concepts in his two fundamental texts *Theosophy* and *Occult Science*![60] So similar and yet so different! It is evident that Rudolf Steiner basically tried to tear asunder the rigid connection between word and concept in such a way that the reader must continually rediscover the meaning of the concepts from their respective contexts.

Thus, on the one hand, he repeatedly uses different terms for seemingly identical facts (for example, in *Occult Science, An Outline* he calls the Atlantean age the Atlantean development, period, epoch, and time.) On the other hand, he uses the same term for differing concepts. He sometimes uses the term "picture" more in the sense of "copy" (for example, when he speaks of the picture quality of thinking).[61] Other times he understands "pictorial" as something in motion, connected with the will, in the sense of the imaginative—for example, when he points out that the verb is always more "pictorial" than the noun.[62]

In Contradiction and between Things

Rudolf Steiner was able to depict personalities and facts from so many different sides that he was accused of self-contradiction even during his own lifetime. Rudolf Steiner often responds to this reproach, perhaps going into the most detail in the preface to the new edition of his *Riddles of Philosophy* in 1924. There he explains: "These things will only be seen correctly if we consider that later works that seem to contradict earlier ones arise out of a spiritual perception of the spiritual world. Those who want to achieve such a perception or who want to maintain it, must develop the capacity of being able to place themselves objectively in the position of what is being observed—suppressing their own sympathies and antipathies. If such a person presents Haeckel's way of thinking, he must be able to immerse himself in it. Precisely through this act of being open to the other does he create the capacity of spiritual perception. The way I present various world views has its origins in my orientation towards a spiritual perception."[63] The presentation of a spiritual truth, of an intrinsic relationship, demands many varied, even seemingly contradictory, observational perspectives: "The individual who has something genuinely clairvoyant to express must work in contradictions, and one contradiction must illuminate others, since the truth lies in the middle."[64]

Rudolf Steiner notes this problem with a concrete example in the two statements, "God is in us," and "We are in God." Each statement is the opposite of the other. Both are true—God is in us and we are in God. "[...] The actual truth, the whole truth, lies in the middle. And the source of all of the argumentation over ideas in the world is based on the fact that people always tend towards a one-sidedness which is true but is nevertheless a one-sided truth, while the actual truth lies between two opposing statements. We must know them both if we want to approach the truth."[65]

Along these same lines, another stylistic approach employed by Rudolf Steiner can often be found through an attentive reading of his work. He attempts to express what he means in the interval between the words, by using several expressions, several concepts. "Through what lies between words with similar sounds, someone who has a lively sense of language [...] can catch hold of ideas for which there is no direct word." He offers the example: The soul lives and weaves. Only through the similar sounds in the concepts of "live" and "weave," by means of what exists in the interval between them, are we able to come close to what is really intended.[66]

In fact, Rudolf Steiner explains that one of spiritual science's stylistic methods is to explain one thing by means of another; for example, to point out the character of the bodily members through their revelation in the course of life. Through this, "the picture quality, the imaginative presentation, is helped in filling abstract words with concrete content. Through comparative presentations, what is abstract becomes concrete and the genius of the language is heard."[67]

Delicate Nuances of the Spiritual

The inner mobility required while reading (or listening) in order to be fully involved in a characterizing style is supported by other stylistic elements—for example, at the level of syntax. In this sense, Rudolf Steiner handles the order of the elements of a sentence—the word order in a sentence—in a rather free way. If we turn our attention to how he begins each sentence, we will quickly note the rich variations with which he does this. We can be certain that there is always a deeper meaning when the order of the elements of a sentence are different than what we expect—at least with the written works; with the lectures, this is not entirely authentic and can often be a bit accidental. Why does he begin the first chapter of *How Do We Achieve Knowledge of Higher Worlds?* with "There slumber in every human being capacities ..." instead of "In every human being slumber capacities ..."? What changes when we change the beginning of *Occult Science* from "An old phrase, 'occult science' will be used for the content of this book" to the more common, "For the content of this book, the old phrase 'occult science' will be used."[68]

In one of his lectures on public speaking[69], Rudolf Steiner points out that a speaker can use unconventional sentence structure and phraseology to "grab the listener by the ear." However, the increased attentiveness that this calls forth, the effect of being pulled out of a kind of automatic thinking, is only one aspect. What is more significant is that delicate nuances of the spiritual require a specific word order. From a spiritual point of view, it makes a difference whether part of a sentence opens a statement, or whether it is in the middle or the end of the sentence. Rudolf Steiner often emphasizes how important it is that the German language offers this freedom of word placement—compared, for example, to French or English.[70]

Closely connected with this is the often complicated syntax that distinguishes Rudolf Steiner's language, and that stands in sharp contrast to our own modern scientific language which strives for the most compactly built sentences through the use of many noun constructions. What actually happens as a result? In order to give an apt example of this, we can cite a German linguist on this subject: "The advantage of this typically German method of construction is the resulting scant use of subordinate clauses; hence, through its form, a relief from the hypotactic multi-dimensionality brought by compound sentences."[71] Each of us could test for ourselves how to rectify this compact, but basically syntactically simple sentence ("The advantage ... is ... the scant use) by means of subordinate clause constructions. We can observe, for example, how Rudolf Steiner introduces the description of the Saturn evolution in *Occult Science*—one sentence that goes on for seven lines and many subordinate clauses of various levels, many insertions, and so forth.

Understanding the Active Spirit through Participation

From this, we can also understand the following statement by Rudolf Steiner: "Therefore, anyone who wants to present something from spiritual science must be particularly careful to avoid abstract concepts, because, through them, he deviates from what he actually wants to say. And a special approach is important here: softening how we express something, not using sharp-edged expressions. A drastic example of this. For me, it is unpleasant in certain circumstances to say, 'A pale person is standing there.' That is painful. On the other hand, something actually starts to breathe reality if I say, 'There is a person who is pale.' When we characterize the fact not with a rigid, simple concept, but with the concept that circulates around it. And we will find that children have much more understanding inwardly for relative things than they do for relationships expressed only in nouns and modifiers."[72] Here we can again recommend a test in which we feel inwardly the difference between saying, "a pale person" or "a person who is pale." We see in this that the "stilted redundance of the sentences" (Beat Wyss) is thoroughly thought out and meaningful.[73]

The last sentence of this citation draws attention to the fact that in the characteristic elements of style described here even the kinds of words play a role, since completely differentiated qualities reside in them: "What emerges from the spirit cannot speak well in nouns. Because the spirit is not active in what nouns are. The spirit is in constant motion. The spirit is thoroughly of the nature of the verb. It dissolves the quality of the noun and prefers to create a subordinate clause rather than a noun."[74] Thus the person who is speaking and listening is more inwardly active when using interjections, prepositions, and verbs; more mobile than when using adjectives or nouns[75], because—and this cannot be stressed often enough—this is simply the sign of good reading and listening: "Our listening, especially in regard to words expressing activity, is actually always a participation. Initially, what is most spiritual in the human being participates; it just refrains from the outer activity itself."[76]

"... a style that can be presented fully in pictures ..."

The Pictorial Element in the Language

"We are insufficiently aware that a language is, in fact, merely symbolic, merely figurative, never a direct expression of the objective world, but only a reflection of it."[77] This was Goethe's critical reflection on the relationship between language and object towards the end of his *Theory of Color*. It is a serious warning to the reader not to mistake the word for the thing itself, and not to let the pictorial nature of language slip from consciousness! It was Goethe—who could handle language in such a sovereign way—that knew how difficult it is "to refrain from replacing the thing with its sign, to keep the object alive before us instead of killing it with the word."[78]

A Cautious, Provisional Allusion

Like Goethe, Rudolf Steiner was also tireless in his attempts to remind his listeners that the most we can do is to *approach* a thing with the help of language, that the word—as used today—can never reach, envelop, encompass, or exhaust the thing itself. Consequently, Steiner used language so that his readers or listeners always had to remain conscious of the character of language itself as mere allusion. Many readers of Steiner's lecture transcripts will have noticed, for instance, how often Rudolf Steiner uses the formulation "I might say."[79] With him, this should not be viewed as a cliché, filler, or verbal pause; instead, this always indicates that a provisional, approximate expression will follow that cannot be taken literally or as the final word. When, for instance, we read: "If we want to arrive at anthroposophy, we must—I might say—learn language anew."[80] Naturally, this does not mean that we must go through the whole process of acquiring language from the beginning. And yet, as anthroposophists, we must learn a new kind of language, a different way of cultivating language—somehow (get to) know language anew. It is not a matter of cultivating a "lexical" connection to words as mere content because "Today, a person who receives a word very quickly finds—I might say—a sort of lexical connection to this word; he looks for a kind of word explanation in order to avoid as much as possible entering into the thing itself."[81]

When I anticipated the core of this statement by putting the word "lexical" in quotation marks—a word Rudolf Steiner once again introduces with a careful "I might say"—I was using a stylistic tool often used by Rudolf Steiner. In his written works, in which he could hardly put an "I might say" in front of merely "approximate" conceptual terms, he used quotation marks which normally point to an "unusual word usage." In Rudolf Steiner's writings, there are quite a few quotation marks to warn the reader of the need for a cautious, provisional understanding.

Speaking Comparatively
Preserves the Intrinsic Character of a Thing

Perhaps we might call this effort by Rudolf Steiner a quest for an "approximate" language. He once remarked about himself that he tried to translate tightly woven concepts into loosely woven concepts.[82] Of course, this refers quite concretely to a certain lecture cycle—namely his art history lectures with slides—but this tendency, this search for "loosely woven" concepts, the avoidance of tightly knit definitions, is found throughout all his works.

Instead of "approximate speaking" we could also call this style "comparative speaking." For Rudolf Steiner often uses *similes*, "illustratively [setting] something alongside."[83]

The stylistic means of simile and metaphor offer deeper access to a thing by throwing a new, often surprising light on the subject. A simile helps us bear in mind—if we are sensitive enough—that the things being compared are not completely identical, that a distance remains, that two things are in agreement only *in regard to a certain quality*. But this distance disappears in the metaphor which brings things consciously together in some respect.

Interestingly, Rudolf Steiner uses almost no metaphors despite his markedly pictorial language. Why? I think it is because he attaches importance to remaining always conscious of the distance between the word and the thing, never allowing us to forget that any speech can only be approximate, pictorial, symbolic. In other words, where Rudolf Steiner uses images, he does not mean them in the sense of "transliteration," but in the sense of dynamically "penetrating a thing with our hearing"—he aims not at the meaning content of the images but at the *inner movement of the image*, the etheric gesture that originally had been (is?) connected with a word.

An example may illustrate and expand on this. In *The Riddle of Man*, we read about a German philosopher: "With Hegel, 'I think, therefore I am' seems to be revived in the evolution of the German worldview like a seed that falls on the earth and grows to become a spreading tree. For what this thinker created as a worldview is a comprehensive thought-painting or something like a many-membered thought-body consisting of numerous individual thoughts that carry, support, move, enliven, illuminate one another."[84]

First note the simile of the seed: the tiny seed corn disappears in the earth and arises as a mighty spreading tree. The inner movement of the image connected with this (something small first disappears fully from view and then arises as something big) can be applied to the thought "I think, therefore I am" which—grown to enormous size—reappears, re-arises through Hegel.

Now Rudolf Steiner characterizes Hegel's worldview further: it "is a comprehensive thought-painting." Again an image. What is the quality of this image? At first we might be inclined to speak of it as a metaphor. But is it really a metaphor?—The ancient rhetorician Quintilian understood metaphor to be an abbreviated simile in which the comparison indicator is left out ("her cornflower eyes" instead of "her eyes as blue as cornflowers"). But Rudolf Steiner is always concerned to keep the comparison indicator as part of the comparison in order to emphasize its character as a simple comparison rather than suppressing that character.

What does he mean when he speaks of "thought-painting?" Doesn't he mean that Hegel's worldview looks something like the painting of thoughts? When we read this metaphorically, we perhaps imagine a framed painting on the wall and then carry this image over into Hegel's worldview. But I don't think Steiner means it in this way; for then he would have added a comparison indicator or a "to some extent." He did not do this—which indicates that we should read "thought-painting" as quite etherically real, as a spiritually appropriate term, so to speak. Hegel's worldview *is* a thought-painting; it *is* a complex, interlinked tableau of concept forms. If we do not take the word "painting" here as a fixed image, but as a gesture, as a living concept, as the movement of a tableau that arises and is built of various elements—then we enter into a sphere of the word that can be called "imaginative."

The Original, Etheric Word Gesture

To characterize what is meant here more fully, I will cite a further example often noted by Rudolf Steiner, which may allow us to make this distinction even clearer. The word "concept"[85] or the verb "conceive" is normally not heard today as a metaphor (in the above sense) [related to its Latin root *capere* (to grasp)–trans.]. I would compare the mental process of understanding with the process of physically grasping—thus making our own—and then carry this image over into the word "concept." But if we follow Rudolf Steiner here, he does not base the formation of this word on a simile: "The concept 'concept' was formed at a time when there was still a living sense of the etheric body that takes hold of things. At that time people were really able to form the concept 'concept' because taking hold with the physical body is just a picture of taking hold with the etheric body."[86] Most of our words were formed at a time when people still had this living perception of the ether body: "Just as my hand is part of me, just as I use it to gesture, the speaker in earlier times felt in the movement and life of the word something like a gesture, a gesture of his air man, his elemental man, within himself."[87] Words did not just arise out of physical perception and comparison, are not just transliterations (= metaphors) from the physical world into the intellect, but are spoken forms that echo an etheric process.

From this standpoint, too, we can understand why Rudolf Steiner so often makes us aware of the original image character in words: the graphic etheric element expressed in the forming of the word can once again be experienced, be felt: "The main point is learning to grasp language as gesture."[88]

Thus when Rudolf Steiner seems to be using a metaphor, we must be especially observant: for the most part, this will be meant in the above sense as spiritual (etheric)—thus real! If this is not the case, he uses a simile—and thus makes us aware of this through a comparison indicator. If we now come back to the Hegel example given above, we will note that Hegel's worldview is further compared with a "thought-body"—but once again a limiting "something like" is inserted that warns us to be careful in how we understand it. The simile "thought-body" is only valid in a particular respect, only "something like."

The Example with Something Left Over

We will find a similar tendency if we look more closely at how Rudolf Steiner uses examples. As far as I have been able to discover, there is often "something left over." Something about them "doesn't quite fit." And that is—in my view—intentional; this is a way to avoid identifying the example (meant only to demonstrate and clarify something particular) with the thing. Here, too, Rudolf Steiner is mainly interested in the inner movement, the etheric gesture that we carry out in connection with an example—and not in forming a fixed, concrete, limited idea that we then identify with the actual subject.

An example of "example:" I have long struggled with the examples Rudolf Steiner uses in the Sound Eurythmy Course to illustrate the character of the iamb and the trochee. For the iamb he gives: "On mountains flaming fire;" for the trochee he gives: "Bring me water below."[89] If we consider the rhythmic form of the sentences—and the rhythm is the point—this at first seems quite unsatisfactory. In the first phrase, the iambs violate the borders of the words—and thus are not completely "full" iambs. The phrase also ends catalectically, i.e., with an incomplete verse foot, with an unstressed syllable that is not followed by a stressed one. Now we might ask: Couldn't Rudolf Steiner have found a better example in the rich abundance of German literature? —The situation is even "worse" in the example of the trochee: There is only *one* nice classical trochee, at the beginning. It is followed by a dactyl—and then the phrase also finishes catalectically, i.e., with a long not followed by a short.

Only after a time did I realize how brilliantly the two

phrases are formed to grasp the *inner character* of iamb and trochee: if we follow the inner gestures of the words, we will hardly find more fitting words to express the "striving," "approaching," "intent to reach" of the iambic, and the measured quiet, the "arriving" element of the trochaic. In each word of the iambic example, a movement is inwardly aroused that goes from below to above: on, mountains, flaming, fire. It is significant that the fiery element striving upward stands at the midpoint here!— On the other hand, we have the water in the phrase for the trochee—and accordingly we have three quiet word gestures that flow downward and spread out below: bringing, water, below.

When we participate in these word movements with inner feeling, we have experienced the *quality of the iamb*, the *quality of the trochee*. In comparison to this inner characterization, it is absolutely secondary whether or not the corresponding rhythm in the examples is maintained with mathematical rigor.

Spiritual Activity in the Emergence of the Image

A further aspect will be characterized briefly here: Rudolf Steiner's increasingly frequent use of blackboard drawings during his lectures over the years is connected with the quest for a pictorial quality we have noted.[90] In these blackboard drawings he was mainly concerned with the gestures that became visible in the movement of drawing, and that his audience could follow during the process of their creation. This becomes particularly perceptible in the drawing for the lecture of June 10, 1924, during the Agricultural Course. This drawing was to demonstrate to the participants the inner quality of being for carbon, for oxygen, for nitrogen. In the way Rudolf Steiner applied each successive color to the blackboard, these qualities could be revealed to the listener or observer who participated inwardly in the movement.[91] In the only known lecture passage where Rudolf Steiner talks about the use of blackboard drawings, there is a clear statement of what he intended with them: "If we really want to progress spiritually, we must always be mindful of taking what we receive from the world and working it through. Therefore, a person will be more successful in attaining to the spiritual element if, in the future, he avoids as much as possible letting the world come to him like a film in a theater. He needs to participate quite a bit in the thinking when he hears about the world. And, as you see, I have not shown you a film, […] but I have made drawings for you that arose in the moment; there you could see what I mean with every stroke; there you could participate in the thinking. This is also an element that needs to enter into our education of children today: the fewest possible finished drawings, the most possible drawings created in the moment, where the child can see every stroke as it arises. In this way the child participates inwardly and thus human beings are roused to inner activity which then makes it possible to live more into the spiritual element and acquire understanding for the spiritual."[92]

Rudolf Steiner's thoroughly pictorial language—in the sense of a moving, dynamic image quality—has many aspects which could only be hinted at here. Rudolf Steiner strove for a style "that can be presented fully in pictures"—as he once noted in relation to one of his book that at first glance seems to be abstract and dry, *The Three-fold Social Order*; for: "whoever wants to be honest with our age will consciously strive for such a style." But he was under no illusions: "Today, if someone develops such a style based entirely on pictorial imaginations, he will normally be told: people don't understand that; it is difficult to understand."[93]

"... so that their content can never be entirely fathomed ..."

On Forming and Experiencing the Mantras

Rudolf Steiner tried to speak and to write so as to help his audience and readers avoid the objective ideas that usually rise up in them a split-second after they hear a word. Instead, the gesture of a word could sound through and the individual would be stimulated to experience language again in a living way.

This is a capacity we need to acquire once again because today we are often completely fixated on the meaning of the word. Feeling, experiencing language as an organism, experiencing the characteristic qualities of language, are entirely lost in the process. Through this, however, we actually become removed from language. With texts that are meant to convey mere information—instruction manuals, for example—a mode of reading directed purely to the content may be appropriate. However, artistically shaped language, or language with a soul-spiritual content, is not suited to this method: "In relation to language, modern consciousness lives completely in the perception of ideas; it has almost completely lost the sense of the sound and the word. But in the perception of ideas, the sense perceptible spirituality that is characteristic of all art is also lost."[94]

Everything in the Verses has Meaning

If we now seek to enter into Rudolf Steiner's non-prose writings (the meditative verses, mantras, the *Mystery Dramas*) we will quickly note that all of the characteristic elements of style found in his other writings appear here in a condensed form—complemented by still other means of linguistic creativity.

These verses by Rudolf Steiner are a cosmos unto themselves; every verse, every mantra must be viewed differently. Thus universal generalizations cannot be set forth here but, instead, a few examples will be examined concretely.

Let us set before our souls the following two (dedicatory) verses by Rudolf Steiner:[95]

Search in the surroundings of the world
And you find yourself as human being
Search within your own human interior
And you find the world

Suche im Umkreis der Welt
Und du findest dich als Mensch,
Suche im eignen menschlichen Innern
Und du findest die Welt.

The human being, when he knows himself
Finds His selfhood becomes the world
The human being, when he knows the world
Finds the world becomes his selfhood.

Erkennt der Mensch sich selbst:
Wird ihm das Selbst zur Welt;
Erkennt der Mensch die Welt:
Wird ihm die Welt zum Selbst.

Thematically and in terms of the content, these two verses seem quite similar; even the same central concepts arise— human being, world. But how differently are they formed! While in the first verse, the dark-sounding *u* that offers direction is decisive, the second is based completely in the sounding of the distancing *e*. While the first has a falling rhythm, the second rises iambically. The tendency of the first verse is to go outward—in the surroundings of the world; and, in the second, the human being is the point of departure. The first verse begins with the will and the direct command "search;" the second verse is concerned with knowing, reflected in the distancing and observant declarative form. The first is based entirely in the tension of "search" and "find"—activity and fulfillment; what takes place in the second verse occurs in the verbs— know and become—with a more qualitative transformation from within.

While those who read these two verses superficially, who view them only casually, could think that they are concerned with the same thing, the person who enters into the verses more sensitively and livingly, experiences two completely different processes, two finely differentiated soul events. With these two verses, we can already have a sense for understanding what Rudolf Steiner once said about the mantras that he gave: "Such verses are not contrived by the will of an individuality; but they are brought forth from the spiritual world. Thus much more is contained in them than is usually believed to be the case. And we think rightly about them when we assume we cannot fully fathom their content, that we will instead always find more in them the more we immerse ourselves in them."[96]

Everything in these mantras is meaningful: the word order and placement of the clauses, the rhythms that move the soul in completely different ways, the change of perspective, and the sounds. The last two aspects play a special role in the mantras.

The Dynamic of the Change in Perspective

For a deeper experience of the mantras it is particularly meaningful for us to participate actively in their inner dynamic. One part of this is immersing ourselves in sensing from which "place in the world," and in what relation to the one meditating, a mantra is spoken: Does it begin on the outside and work its way inward? Who is speaking? Does the direction reverse? Is the mantra in the first person-, in the second person-, or the third person-singular? Does the perspective change over the course of the mantra? What is question; what is statement; what is depiction; what is request? Must different parts of the mantra be heard differently?

These are just some of the questions, exercises, tasks that can arise in connection with a mantra. This inner mobility can also be practiced with good poems, in most of which several changes of perspective occur. Fairytales, however, are especially suited to this sensing of the inner course, the inner dynamic.—If these exercises are done often, it will soon be noted how differently one has learned to understand the mantras, by which is meant that one has learned to sense them differently; has trained the capacity to be able to observe how various perspectives and movements come together in the soul as a complete "dynamic tableau." We can understand from this what Rudolf Steiner says about the meaning of Frau Balde's fairytales for Professor Capesius (two characters in Rudolf Steiner's *Mystery Dramas*): "For Capesius, fairytales are what bring about imaginative knowledge. Not what is contained in them, what they relate, but *how they progress, how one portion is related to another—this is what lives and weaves in his soul.* The one part allows certain soul forces to strive upwards, another part allows others to strive downwards, and still other forces come to cross through the motion of these forces striving upward and downward. Through this he comes into motion within his soul; through this what finally permits him to see into the spiritual world is brought forth from his soul."[97] The point is to move along with this course of things, this inner dynamic—and, as a result, to experience it first-hand.

Sound and the Feeling of Sound

Sounds are another central element in the formation of mantric verses. Rudolf Steiner often points out that today sounds have come to be understood as only accidental signs and that we no longer have any natural sense for their inner quality. He asked again and again that we develop an *understanding for sound*, a *feeling for sound*, that we learn to *hear* sounds. He offers examples in many of his lectures of how we should learn to feel our way into the word or into its sounds.

One example that is sometimes given is the word *Zweifel* [doubt]. Who, he asks, "feels in the word *Zweifel* that the word *Zwei* [two] is in it, that we stand opposite a thing which is divided in two? Who has any feeling at all for this *zw, z-w*? Everywhere *zw* appears, we have the same feeling that arises with *Zweifel*—as though the thing divides in two. *Zwischen* [between]—you have the same thing! *Zweck, Zweifel, zwar* [goal, doubt, but]—try to feel it! Feeling can rest in all the relationships of sounds."[98] We can grow into the pictorial quality of language—and thus into the pictorial sphere of our own soul as well—through just this kind of sensitivity to the sound. In this way, we can come to sense the genius of the language.

The sound acquires a particular weight in the mantras. At the place where the author is linguistically creative— and, with genuine mantras, this cannot be any other way—he is shifted back to the primal source of word formation where sound content and meaning content are completely one, where every sound is in its place out of an inner necessity.[99] In connection with this, Rudolf Steiner often refers to the seventh scene of the Mystery Drama *The Portal of Initiation:* "Thus I sought to indicate the intrinsic character of words and sounds throughout the secrets of the cosmos. By doing this, much could be made audible to the ear which, expressed in modern words, sounds abstract. People must listen to the sounds of the words, how the correct sound stands in the correct place. You must feel where it does and does not belong. That is like a spiritual alchemy. And the interweaving and intermingling of the spiritual forces in the cosmos can be indicated through such means."[100] As a result, however, we come to a completely different level of experience: "There is a different kind of understanding than what can be achieved through words. Language, in its sounds, is really a vastly wondrous instrument. It is much, much cleverer than human beings, and we would do well to listen to its wisdom."[101]

Creating Words Anew from the Feeling for the Sounds

Thus it depends on feeling the sound again—[on the] "ego feeling as though it is going through the sounds"[102]—and, as a result, on schooling a feeling for language, a conscientiousness with language. It is a matter of "making the understanding of sound active in ourselves once again […] of making the sound as such active within ourselves."[103] Eurythmy and speech formation offer wonderful assistance in developing this understanding for sounds, this feeling for sounds, which seems quite foreign to us today.

In the mantra each sound needs its specific qualities and its place in the word—as well as in the verse—to be intimately felt. Otherwise, we would never be able to work our way through to the inner character of the mantra. Merely intellectual, content-related observations lead us away from it instead.

It is precisely from this importance of the sounds that we can come to understand how the words of a language, the vocabulary of a language, are inadequate to express the most delicate nuances. It is here that the spiritual researcher, according to Rudolf Steiner, is often compelled to take up creating new words: "Today one is hardly forgiven when he wants to bring life into the language. I have actually tried it in my writing in very homeopathic doses. You see, simply in order to make certain things sensory, I needed a concept in my writings, a concept for something that has the same relationship to *Kraft* [power] as flowing water in the stream has to an icy surface that has formed on it. I used the verb *kraften*. As a rule, German has only the noun *Kraft*; it does not have a verb *kraften*."[104]

In the meditative verses in *Truth Wrought Words* and the *Mystery Dramas*, we find a new and completely different kind of word formation. Rudolf Steiner makes abundant use of the special capacity of the German language to create compounds—not only the (more common) two word compounds, but often three-word compounds: *Tatergießen* [deed flood], *Weltenwalten* [world wielding], *Weltenwesenwacht* [world-being-watch], *Lebenswirkensmacht* [life-working-power] (from *The Twelve Moods*); *Welten-Keimesworte* [world-seed-words], *Seelengründe* [soul-foundations], *Geisteskleid* [spirit-raiment], *Zeitenfinsternis* [ages-darkness] (from *The Calendar of the Soul*); *Mondenlichtgeflimmer* [moon-light-glimmer], *Lebenshoffnungstrank* [life's-hope-draught], *Nixen-Wechselkräfte* [nixie-transformation-powers] (from the *Mystery Dramas*); *Wurzelwesenskraft* [root-being-power], *Feuerstrebekraft* [fire-striving-power] (from the *Elemental Beings* verse).

What happens when such complex word structures are created? At first we lose some of the solid earth beneath our feet because we are unable to connect any concrete ideas with these words. Certainly with their individual parts— but in combination, their meaning becomes blurred. How can such a word be read at all? Take *Wurzelwesenskraft*—is that the power of a root being? Or is it the elemental power of the root? There is nothing definitive in it to connect to a single meaning.—Based on my own experience, we make the most progress here when—supported by the sound—we seek out the gestures of the word. When these two are combined, a "word painting" results that leads in the direction Rudolf Steiner intended. Let us try this with the word "Wurzelwesenskraft:" *Wurzel* [root] can be felt as something that condenses itself, contracts, hides, goes into the depths. *Wesen* [being] as something quite inward, quite individual, quite essential—"the very essence of being." *Kraft* [power] is something that works outwards as a capacity to form. If we look at these three words together, a "picture" results of something that works outward (*Kraft*), that combines the capacity of densification, of contraction, of arriving at what is essential—the power of the gnomes. Let us look at *Feuerstrebekraft* alongside this: the strong fricative *f* leads us outwards; the *eu* leads us into the heights; *strebe* repeats this movement, but leads by means of the *str* (*hinstrahlende Energie* [radiating energy])[105] with somewhat more purpose, more form. In summary, something that is active (*Kraft*) that leads purposefully into the heights (*Feuerstrebe*).—Naturally, in a next step, these compounds must be connected with the whole gesture of the sentence where they become more finely nuanced.

Inexhaustible Word Combinations

One last thing should be said here that plays a role not only with the mantras but is often found elsewhere in Rudolf Steiner's work. It is what I would call the creation of *dy-*

namic series, of serial intensifications. If, for example, we look back at the discussion of Hegel's worldview in the last essay, it says there that this is "to a certain extent, a many-membered body of thought comprised of a multitude of individual thoughts that mutually *carry, support, move, enliven, illuminate* one another.[106] What a series! Carry, support, move, enliven, illuminate—that is not an accidental listing of verbs or even synonyms. Instead, there is a development that can be seen in the course of the series. "Support" is more active than "carry;" with "move" this activity is heightened—the "individual thoughts" now exert a dynamic influence on one another; "enliven"—here, an inherent life is kindled from within, which then experiences a further intensification in "illuminate" when a (light) effect now becomes visible even from outside.

These intensifications—and the inner penetration of what has been heightened, metamorphosed, transformed—are quite essential to an understanding and experience of the inner nature of mantras. And so, in closing, a mantric verse, *To One Who Understands the Sense of Language,* will be offered as an example. Rudolf Steiner gave this verse to the first Waldorf teachers of classical languages, and this intensification can easily be followed in it.— Let us sense sequentially the words in the verse below: "*enthüllen, erschließen, beschenken, verleihen*" [reveal, open, bestow, lend]. What I "reveal" I already see in its own form, but only in its outer aspect. In "opening" I arrive at what lies within. Someone who bestows something on me gives me something of himself which then, in "lend," is infinitely intensified—a capacity, an ability is lent.—Thus this verse makes quite evident what Rudolf

Steiner once said about the quality of mantras in general: "We would have to write many books if we wanted to exhaust the full meaning of these verses; for not only is every word meaningful in them, but also the symmetry of the words, the way they are distributed, the intensifications within them, and much more, so that only long and patient dedication to these things will exhaust what is contained in them."[107]

To one who understands the sense of language
The world unveils itself
In image.

To one who hears the soul of language
The world opens itself
As Being.

To one who lives the spirit of language
The world gives the gift
Of Wisdom's power.

To one who can feel love of language
Language lends
Its own strength.

So will I turn heart and mind
To the spirit and soul
Of the word;

And in my love for it
I feel myself
Now whole

Wer der Sprache Sinn versteht,
Dem enthüllt die Welt
Im Bilde sich.

Wer der Sprache Seele hört,
Dem erschließt die Welt
Als Wesen sich.

Wer der Sprache Geist erlebt,
Den beschenkt die Welt
Mit Weisheitskraft;

Wer die Sprache lieben kann,
Dem verleiht sie selbst
Die eigne Macht.

So will ich Herz und Sinn
Nach Geist und Seele
Des Wortes wenden;

Und in der Liebe
Zu ihm mich selber
Erst ganz empfinden.

"Rising to the level of the process through which language is created …"
Spiritual Scientific Language as a Work of Art

In his discussions of language, Rudolf Steiner pursues different goals than is generally the case in such matters. For him it is not a question of clothing thoughts in easily understood words; it is not a matter of turning slick phrases or playing indulgently with language. It is also not a matter of becoming known as a popular author. He was concerned with something else entirely. His books were meant to be "awakeners of spiritual life within the reader." Reading them should "not merely be a matter of reading text, but should be an experience with inner surprises, tensions, and resolutions."[108]

He was quite conscious of how difficult, how virtually insoluble the task of this sort of writing is. And so he wrote about his struggle, "I know that what I have presented in my books falls short of triggering such an experience in these reading souls through its own forces. But I also know how, with every page, my inner battle was focused on accomplishing as much as possible in this direction."[109]

And he then describes what he was attempting to do—and how, for example, we can understand why Herman Hesse experienced Steiner's style as "bloodless"[110]: "In regard to style, I do not write so that my subjective feeling life can be felt in the sentences. In the process of writing, I hold back what comes out of warmth and a deep feeling so that the style becomes dry, mathematical. But this style alone can be an awakener because the reader must allow warmth and feeling to awaken within himself. The reader, in a passive state of mind, cannot simply allow this to flow over into himself from the presenter."[111]

The Anthroposophical Book—A Kind of Musical Score

Rudolf Steiner's whole effort went into writing so that the individual is stimulated to take up his own thinking. "My *Occult Science* has no content for anyone who does not take up working it out for himself. It is, in a certain respect, only a musical score, and the individual himself must work out its content through his own inner activity. Only then does he have it. Then, as an observer, he will acquire what the spiritual researcher has discovered, […] active thinking, the thinking that immerses itself in reality, that unites itself with reality."[112]

Rudolf Steiner characterizes another of his works similarly—which indicates that the qualities discussed do not belong only to the works mentioned but are qualities of every genuinely spiritual scientific text. "My *Philosophy of Freedom* is intended to make the individual reach for his own direct activity of thought on every page, so that, to a certain extent, the book is itself a kind of musical score and the individual must read this score through an inner activity of thinking in order to progress continually from thought to thought by his own means. Thus, with this book, the mental participation of the reader is always expected."[113]

For this reason, Rudolf Steiner fought against demands to write "more popularly": "I always resisted the notion because it was an essential part of what they [my books] were meant to be that they not be popular. If we pour what is offered in our anthroposophical literature into all manner of confused forms and then want to bring this […] to the public, only complacency will be served, on the one hand, and nonsense put forth on the other. Because nonsense will always arise when the effort is made to consider the spirit in an easy, thoughtless way. The work we are carrying out when we learn to understand a difficult text is an inner training; it contributes to working out our relationship to the spiritual world in the right way."[114]

If we do not develop an understanding for the special and yet deeply necessary form of spiritual scientific presentation; if we are not involved in this inner process, in this "inner training," the presentations can be felt as unscientific—as they were by Wolfgang Müller-El Abd —and a longing arises for "other forms of verification."[115] If we take up Rudolf Steiner's language in the same way we read "scientific presentations", we seek definitions and connect fixed ideas about content with the words. But this is precisely what the spiritual scientific researcher seeks to overcome; he avoids the use of definitions, the use of words as "communication currency."

The Artistic Factor in Spiritual Scientific Literature

The theme of the previous chapters was the special linguistic means Rudolf Steiner employed to stimulate the inner activity of the reader. At the same time, it became clear there that the spiritual researcher uses language in a quite different and, in part, very unusual way. The use of largely forgotten rhetorical means in lectures—like structuring according to the rhythm of speech or pre-positioning the verb—is unusual for modern consciousness. It is uncommon to characterize rather than to define concepts; uncommon always to remain aware of the purely approximate quality of language through the use of comparative formulations. It is uncommon to use as much as possible the relative freedom of word placement in German to achieve delicate nuance; to construct seemingly complicated subordinate clauses based on the verb instead of compact noun constructions; to assign a new, central meaning to sounds; to draw attention to the original meanings of words, to hear the gestures behind them; to use the blackboard not only for didactic purposes but to allow "thought pictures" to arise. And much more.

Along with this, something else comes into consideration that Rudolf Steiner expresses through an interesting comparison in the lecture passages cited earlier. He calls *The Philosophy of Freedom* as well as *Occult Science* "musical scores." An eloquent image! A musical score is the written form of a (tonal-) work which can only sound forth again through a personal transformation of it in the present. A musical score unites individual voices—the essential element only arises as a complete tonal picture in the "composition", in the sounding together of the various voices as one harmony. A musical score is a work of art, an organic whole, in which every detail necessarily stands in a particular place and cannot be moved around at will. This also applies to what Rudolf Steiner strove for stylistically. "What is intended here is something so organically complete in itself that a necessity of form must eventually express itself in the language, in the same way that an earlobe expresses a necessity of form that is inevitable as a result of the form of the whole human being."[116]

And just as with a musical score, the reader undergoes a *process in time*—experiences tensions and release, dramatic passages, the building up of images and then, once again, their dissolution. These join together in a complete work of art, in a kind of "soul tableau" and must then become somehow visible.

The comparison with the musical score is anything but accidental. Writing a spiritual scientific work, holding a spiritual scientific lecture, is *always* an artistic process! And as with every artistic work, with every poetic work, *content and form* are one: "every such sentence [is] a birth … because it has to be experienced inwardly, through the soul, not merely as thought but as immediate form." If, in this sense, we want to write spiritual scientific works, we cannot "create [one] … without an artistic, active sense of the language."[117]

This is the deeper mystery of spiritual scientific literature! It is scientific in that it promises an experience of verification by stimulating the reader's own activity, through independent re-creation. At the same time, it is also artistic in that the form and content coincide. It is not a transmission of truths by means of content; instead, the experience of the truth is constituted in and with the language form through which it is conveyed—it is inseparable from it.[118] Consequently, the same thing applies to genuine spiritual scientific presentation that, in connection with poetry and literature, Goethe, Jean Paul, and Hofmannsthal "had so urgently stressed: in literature—or art—we are dealing with a specific truth that is evident only in the experience of the artistic form and formation; it cannot, however, be abstracted as thought and doctrine."[119] In this sense, Rudolf Steiner also applies a somewhat "literary concept" of presentation in his writing! Thus his descriptions are not intended to be "poetic" in the way that Peter Petersen insinuates;[120] instead, the artistic factor is inherent in them from the very beginning.

Returning to the Source where Language Arises

Here we will give further consideration to something Rudolf Steiner mentions occasionally. The spiritual scientist can only form artistically when he succeeds in "rising to the level of the process through which language is created."[121]"... by silencing what otherwise lives in language—the capacity for ideas and memory [he must arouse within himself] ... the creative powers of language themselves, those creative powers that were active in human evolution when language originated. The seer must place himself into the state of soul where language first arose, must develop the two-fold activity of inwardly forming the spiritual that he observed, and immersing himself in the spirit of language formation so that he is capable of uniting the two."[122] How we are to imagine this becomes clear in the following statement: "He [the seer] gradually arrives at the point of placing himself back into the linguistically creative spirit that reigned before any language had arisen; of living again into the sounds, into the genius of sound; of immersing himself in this with his whole soul being. He sees how a vowel is included, how

76

a vowel flows into this or that language. In order to transport himself back into the linguistically creative condition of the language of his own people the seer has to express himself more through the how than the what."[123]

This is what is significant. The spiritual researcher has to lift himself up and into the linguistically creative sphere; just as he must rediscover the original source where language is first formed in literature and poetry. From this, we can conclude that he must strip away what clings to language in the way of physical reminiscences, expectations, and associations. It as though he must create language anew; he must give back to it the spirit which the conventions of everyday and scientific usage, the inflated and thoughtless use of language, took away from it. Thus he arrives in the sphere where the formation of words becomes meaningful again, where the gesture expressed through the forming of sound is again united with the meaning, with the spiritual essence, with the spiritual, primal image. That is where language once again becomes magical, as it were; it is no longer merely "the currency of communication;" it no longer lives merely in the intellectual realm or information. Instead, it appears once again saturated with a mood of soul and creative power, creative effectiveness.

In regard to the quality of this language created from an experience of the formative realm, we are dealing with an entirely different language than the one we find in use every day. We can understand it when Rudolf Steiner says, "Therefore, it is important to realize that the words of the seer have to be understood differently from other words. The seer must use language when he reports but in such a way that he allows what is creatively active in the language to arise again by entering into the formative forces of language."[124]

The Whitsun Experience of Language in the Future

If we understand this, it also throws light on another, puzzling remark by Rudolf Steiner. Now and then he mentions that "spiritual science [... has] in it the capacity to bring the linguistic element into creative motion. [...] And a time will appear to us in dimensional perspective [...] where language will become creative through what we think and imagine in spiritual science. Insofar as it is true that spiritual science will one day be spread across the whole earth, it is just as true that it will bring forth a common language that corresponds to no current language. [...] The language of the future will arise as a result of human beings learning to live in the sound, in the same way that he can learn to live in color.—When we learn to live in sound, sound gives birth to a situation where the human being recovers the possibility of creating a language again from spiritual experience."[125]

There is no doubt that we are still very, very far away from this Whitsun experience. And yet it is important to know about this, because we can only find the way when we see the goal. "Although we still stand at the beginning in regard to much of spiritual science, in regard to what has just been characterized we are not even at the beginning. But we must think about this in order to sense in the soul the whole significance and essential quality of spiritual science; in order to sense that spiritual science carries in its womb a new knowledge, a new art, and even a new

78

language—a language that will not be made, but born."[126]

Rudolf Steiner tirelessly warns us that surrendering ourselves to language as it is today, allowing language to think for us, as it were, leads into the realm of the counter forces. Emancipation from the language as it exists to-day—understood as arbitrary tokens, hemmed in by conventions—is essential. At the same time, however, it is a matter of fructifying the language anew: the development of living thoughts, imaginative thinking, requires another kind of language, an approach to language in an artistic, experientially involved way. That is not easy to achieve, but a beginning is made when we learn to feel our way into the words again and, from there, develop a feeling for language and a conscience for language.[127]

If we observe how Rudolf Steiner changed his style throughout his life, we see that he traveled his own path—also in relation to language—with increasing consistency.[128] When we occupy ourselves with his language in this sense, we recognize that it cannot be a matter of imitating him, but of penetrating the forms into which he poured his findings, of understanding their spirit, and then developing from these our own re-enlivened style of language appropriate to what is spiritual.

Endnotes

1 PISA 2000, p.80.

2 Goedart Palm: "Die Zukunft des Lesens" [The future of reading], (May 24, 2001),
http://www.heise.de/tp/r4/html/result.xhtml?url=/tp/r4/artikel/7/7719/1.html&words=Zukunft%20des%20Lesens

3 Rudolf Steiner, *Mein Lebensgang* [The course of my life], GA 28, Chapter 33.

4 Lecture of February 3, 1923, GA 259, p. 99.

5 Lecture of October 5, 1922, GA 217, p. 43.

6 Edith Attinger: *Rudolf Steiners "Geheimwissenschaft im Umriß" in modernem Deutsch* [Rudolf Steiner's *Occult Science, an Outline* in modern German], 2001, p. 5.

7 *Die Drei*, Nr. 2 (2002), p. 46.

8 Ibid., p. 48.

9 Ibid., p. 51.

10 Ibid., p. 49.

11 *Die Drei*, Nr. 4 (2002), p. 57.

12 Beat Wyss, *Der Wille zur Kunst. Zur ästhetischen Mentalität der Moderne* [The will to art. On the aesthetic mentality of the modern age] (Cologne, 1996), p. 143.

13 Paul Klee, *Tagebücher* [Diaries], introduced and edited by Felix Klee (Cologne, 1957), p. 387.

14 Ibid., p. 388.

15 Cited in Peter Selg, "Das eigene Blut, Die Leukämie-Erfahrung Rainer Maria Rilkes (I)" ["His own blood, Rainer Maria Rilke's experience with leukemia (I)"] in *Das Goetheanum*, Nr. 26 (2000), p. 536.

16 Cited in Ralf Lienhard, "Hermann Hesse und die Anthroposophie" ["Herman Hesse and anthroposophy"], *Info 3*, Nr. 7–8 (2002), p. 26.

17 This letter was provided to Ralf Lienhard by Suhrkamp Publishers for use in his study, *Hermann Hesse und die Anthroposophie* [Herman Hesse and anthroposophy].

18 Max Brod, "Höhere Welten" ["Higher worlds"], *Pan,* June 16, 1911; cited in *Rudolf Steiner Gesamtausgabe, Eine Dokumentation* [Rudolf Steiner's collected works, A documentation] (Dornach 1988), p. 37.

19 This text appeared in 1914, considerably expanded under the title, *Die Rätsel der Philosophie* [The riddles of philosophy] (GA 18). Reprint of the review by Julius Frisch in *Beiträge zur Rudolf-Steiner-Gesamtausgabe* [Contributions on the collected works of Rudolf Steiner], Nr. 79–80 (1983), pp. 49–54. The citation referred to is on page 54.

20 Nevertheless, Rudolf Steiner himself tells about his childhood that it was "difficult going for me...in everything connected with language, even in German. Up to the time he was 14 or 15 years old that boy made the most foolish mistakes in German in his school work; only the content helped him past the numerous grammatical and orthographic mistakes." He attributed this "lack of consideration for certain grammatical and orthographic relationships in his mother tongue" to the "lack of relationship with the physical body." He had "little sense for the connection between words and things, if the words were not often spoken aloud. But he had a remarkable sense for the sound of words, for what can be heard through the sound of the words." From the autobiographical lecture of February 4, 1913, reprinted in the *Beiträge zur Rudolf-Steiner-Gesamtausgabe* [Contributions on the collected works of Rudolf Steiner], Nr. 83–84 (1984).

21 Lecture of March 17, 1923, in GA 349, p. 94.

22 Cited here according to Uwe Pörksen: *Wissenschaftssprache und Sprachkritik* [Scientific language and linguistic criticism], Tübingen 1994, pp.313f.

23 Rudolf Steiner, Lecture of January 17, 1920, GA 196.

24 Iwan Goll; cited here according to Karlheinz Daniels: *Über die Sprache* [On language], Bremen 1996, p. 249.

25 Rudolf Steiner: *Die Geheimwissenschaft im Umriß* [Occult science, an outline] (GA 13), p. 21.

26 Ibid., p. 55.

27 Rudolf Steiner: *Aus der Akasha-Chronik*, (GA 11), p. 22.

28 Rudolf Steiner: "Sprache und Sprachgeist" [Language and the spirit of language], in: *Der Goetheanumgedanke inmitten der Kulturkrisis* [The idea of the Goetheanum in the crisis of culture] (GA 36), p. 296f.

29 Ibid., p. 297.

30 Rudolf Steiner, Lecture of May 5, 1918, in GA 271, p. 177. Italics by MMS.

31 These specific stylistic approaches used by Rudolf Steiner will be the subject of further investigation in the subsequent essays of this series.

32 Lecture of October 12, 1922, in GA 217, p. 148.

33 Lecture of December 5, 1907, in GA 56, p. 224.

34 Lecture of January 30, 1923, in GA 259, p. 32.

35 Lecture of September 12, 1915, in GA 253, p. 58. Compare with the Esoteric Lesson of September 3 1913 (in GA 266/3) as well as the March 20, 1914 lecture in GA 145.

36 Lecture of December 18, 1910, in GA 122, p. 230.

37 The lecture of April 30, 1923 in GA 84, page 195f.

38 A closer examination shows that these major elements can be further differentiated according to the type of source and the type of text; however, this is only of secondary interest for what we are discussing here.

39 GA 28, *Mein Lebensgang* [The course of my life], Chapter XXXV, p. 444.

40 Ibid., p. 452.

41 Lectures of October 11–16, 1921, in GA 339.

42 Lecture of October 12, 1921, in GA 339, p. 38.

43 *Das Wesen der Anthroposophie* [The nature of anthroposophy] (Dornach, 1998), p. 12. Lecture of January 24, 1922. Here the unedited version (according to the transcription of Walter Vegelahn's stenogram) has been cited in order to make the peculiarities of the oral delivery clear. Marie Steiner lightly edited the lecture for the first edition in

1943. —Literally the sentence reads: "Since anthroposophy takes its departure entirely from a scientific basis/ it had to/—since it was concerned with the great, comprehensive/ riddles of existence of interest to all humanity/—it had to develop/ so that it accommodates an understanding of even the most simple human soul,/ so that it accommodates the practical, modern needs of the human life of soul and spirit/ which seek there inner support for the soul,/ sureness for the soul,/ power to act,/ belief in humanity,/ in human destiny."

44 Cf. for example, the discussion in Peter von Polenz: *Deutsche Sprachgeschichte vom Spätmittelalter bis zur Gegenwart* [German lingistic history from the late middle ages to the present], Vol. II (Berlin, New York, 1994), chapter 5.

45 When Rudolf Steiner actually found time to revise a lecture manuscript for print, "no stone was left standing." (See for example, the lecture of October 1, 1916, in GA 35). He is supposed to have said once, in this regard, that it would be less trouble for him to create a text for publication rather than editing the transcript.—The conscious way he used rhetorical tools is made apparent in an instruction to Adolph Arenson—the first editor of his lectures— which Georg Unger was kind enough to share with me: The verb was to be correctly placed for written German, long sentences were to be revised, all asides to the audience were to be deleted, etc.

46 Lecture of April 16, 1915, in GA 64, p. 448.

47 Lecture of September 21, 1921, in GA 343, p. 57.

48 Lecture of September 13, 1922, in GA 215, p. 129. At most, we find a few notes or main points for his lectures in his notebooks. Whether he had these in front of him when he lectured is unknown.

49 Lecture of May 5, 1918, in GA 271, p. 177.

50 His attempts in this area were later published under the title *Anthroposophie. Ein Fragment* [Anthroposophy. A fragment] (GA 45).

51 Lecture of October 2, 1920, in GA 322, p. 105f.

52 Lecture of November 25, 1919, in GA 297, p. 153.

53 Rudolf Steiner, Lecture of June 16, 1923, in GA 277, p. 342f.

54 Lecture of June 5, 1917, in GA 176, p. 41.

55 Lecture of March 28, 1919, in GA 190.

56 Essay, "Sprache und Sprachgeist" [Language and the spirit of language] (1922), in GA 36, *Der Goetheanum-Gedanke* [The idea of the Goetheanum], p. 300.

57 Cf. especially the lecture of October 12, 1921, in GA 339, in which Rudolf Steiner speaks of three phases of language development or of the relationship between word and concept.

58 Cf. the lecture of June 5, 1917, in GA 176, as well as the lecture of September 18, 1915, in GA 164.

59 Lecture of October 12, 1921, in GA 339.

60 Cf. the chapter *Das Wesen des Menschen* [The nature of the human being] in GA 8, *Theosophie* [Theosophy], and *Vom Wesen der Menschheit* [On the nature of humanity] in GA 13, *Die Geheimwissenschaft im Umriß* [Occult science, an outline].

61 Lecture of June 1, 1922, in GA 83, p. 22f.

62 In the lecture of March 28, 1919, in GA 190. With regard to the use of the word "bildhaft" [pictorial] see also Martina Maria Sam, "'Ein Stil, der vorgestellt werden kann durch und durch in Bildern ...' Die Veranlagung imaginativen Denkens durch Rudolf Steiners Tafelzeichnungen und Sprachstil" [A style that can be presented completely in pictures ... The gift of imaginative thinking brought by Rudolf Steiner's blackboard drawings and linguistic style] in A. Neider/R. Halfen: *Imagination. Das Erleben des schaffenden Geistes* [Imagination, the experience of the creative spirit] (Stuttgart 2002).

63 In GA 18, *Die Rätsel der Philosophie* [The riddles of philosophy], p. 10.

64 Lecture of June 1, 1918, in GA 271, p. 236f.

65 Lecture of January 21, 1921, in GA 203, p. 89f.

66 Lecture of December 31, 1919, in GA 299, p. 51.

67 Lecture of March 28, 1919, in GA 190, p. 69.

68 The strength of the inner linguistic experience as a result of word order can be tested through familiar poems. How much would C. F. Meyer's poem *Roman Fountain* lose if, instead of "Up rises the spray," it said "The spray rises up" which sounds more normal to the prosaic ear.

69 Lecture of October 16, 1921, in GA 339.

70 Cf. for example, the lectures of March 14, 1915, in GA 159, and March 23, 1919, in GA 190.

71 Peter von Polenz, *Deutsche Sprachgeschichte vom Spätmittelalter bis zur Gegenwart, Band II*, [History of the German language from the late middle ages to the present, volume 2], p. 272.

72 Lecture of July 24, 1924, in GA 311, p. 148.

73 See p. 81, footnote 12.

74 Lecture of March 14, 1921, in GA 338, p. 106.

75 In particular, he points to this phenomenon when he speaks about communication with the dead. According to Rudolf Steiner, after death, they very quickly lose the capacity to understand nouns, while they are able to "understand" verbs and interjections for a long time. (Cf. for example, the lecture of March 28, 1919, in GA 190.)

76 Lecture of August 25, 1919, in GA 294, p. 61. In this pedagogical lecture, Rudolf Steiner goes more fully into the qualities of the noun (separating), the adjective (drawing closer together), and the verb (uniting).

77 J. W. von Goethe, *Theory of Color,* "Concluding Observation on Language and Terminology," in *Scientific Studies*, ed. and trans. Douglas Miller (Suhrkamp Publishers: New York, 1988), p.277.

78 Ibid. Cf. also Uwe Pörksen, "Alles ist Blatt. Über die Reichweite und Grenzen der naturwissenschaftlichen Sprache und Darstellungsmodelle Goethes [All is leaf. On the extent and limits of Goethe's natural scientific language and modes of presentation], *Wissenschaftssprache und Sprachkritik* [Scientific language and language criticism] (Tübingen, 1994), p. 109–130.

79 Rudolf Steiner also often uses the words "to some extent" and "so to speak" in the same sense. Or he avoids a direct term and circumscribes the thing with "that which" etc.

80 Lecture of March 17, 1923, in GA 349, p. 94.

81 Lecture of June 13, 1923, in GA 258, p. 84.

82 Lecture of January 21, 1917, in GA 174, p, 214.

83 Lecture of May 6, 1918, in GA 271, p. 202.

84 GA 20, *Vom Menschenrätsel* [On the riddle of the human being], p. 46.

85 The German word is *Begriff*, literally "what is grasped."

86 Lecture of October 12, 1921, in GA 339, p. 34.

87 Lecture of March 28, 1915, in GA 161, p. 192 f.

88 Lecture of October 17, 1918, in GA 277a, p. 368.

89 Cf. the lecture of July 4, 1924, in GA 279.

90 This theme is discussed in detail in Martina Maria Sam: *Bildspuren der Imagination* [Pictorial traces of the imagination] (Dornach, 2000). An analysis of blackboard drawings from this standpoint can also be found in the article: "Ein Stil, der vorgestellt werden kann durch und durch in Bildern ... [A style that can be presented fully in pictures ...] in Andreas Neider and Roland Halfen, *Imagination. Das Erleben des schaffenden Geistes* [Imagination. The experience of the creative spirit] (Stuttgart, 2002).

91 A detailed discussion of this blackboard drawing is found in the two books cited in the previous footnote. (pp. 47–51; pp. 95–97).

92 Lecture of July 18, 1923, in GA 350, p. 206f.

93 Lecture of March 28, 1919, in GA 190, p. 65.

94 From "Aphoristische Ausführungen über Sprachgestaltung ..." [Aphoristic discussions of speech formation] in GA 280, p. 213.

95 From *Wahrspruchworte* [Truth wrought words] (GA 40), p. 290 and 288. Rudolf Steiner dedicated the first verse to Anna Samweber, the second to Elisabeth Vreede. This dedication to particular personalities surely plays an important role in the forming of the verses.

96 Esoteric lesson of October 24, 1905, in GA 266/1. It

should be remembered that there is no stenographic transcript of these words; instead, they are notes taken from memory by participants.

97 Lecture of December 19, 1917, in GA 127, p. 207 (italics mine, MMS).

98 Lecture of June 5, 1917, in GA 176, p. 41.

99 Cf., for example, the discussion of the spiritual secrets in the sounds of the mantra "It thinks me—It weaves me—It produces me," in the esoteric lessons for 1913 in GA 266/3.

100 Lecture of December 18, 1910, in GA 124, p. 232.

101 ibid., p.230f.

102 Lecture of June 24, 1924, in GA 311, p. 145.

103 Lecture of September 29, 1921, in GA 343, p. 136.

104 Lecture of May 5, 1920, in GA 301, p. 165.

105 Cf. Rudolf Steiner's explanations of the name "Strader" in: Max Gümbel-Seiling, "Einige Erinnerungen an die Mysterienspiele in München" in: *Deutsche Mitteilungen*, Nr. 7/1949 [Some memories of the Mystery plays in Munich, in the Newsletter of the German Anthroposophical Society].

106 From GA 20, p. 46.

107 Report on the Theosophical Congress of 1907, in GA 284, p. 40 f.

108 GA 28, Chapter XXXIII, p. 435f.

109 Ibid.

110 See Ralf Lienhard, „Hermann Hesse und die Anthroposophie," [Hermann Hesse and anthroposophy] *Info 3*, 2002, no. 7–8.

111 See note 108.

112 Lecture of May 4, 1920, in GA 334, p. 244.

113 Lecture of October 3, 1920, in GA 322, p. 111.

114 Lecture of September 12, 1915, in GA 253, p. 58.

115 Guest commentary by Wolfgang Müller-El Abd in *Die Drei* 2002, Nr. 2.

116 Lecture of October 12, 1921, in GA 339, p. 43.

117 Lecture of January 20, 1910, in GA 59, p. 39.

118 One might be reminded here of Paul Klee who once wrote of his artistic work that he was attempting to set forth paths in the picture so that it was not so much what was formed (final form) but the process of forming (initial form) that could be experienced in the work of art. See Jürg Spiller, *Paul Klee. Das bildnerische Denken*, [Paul Klee, thinking in pictures], (Basel, Stuttgart, 1964), vol. 2, p. 269.

119 Wolfgang Kayser, *Die Wahrheit der Dichter* [The poets' truth], (Hamburg, 1959), p. 52.

120 Peter Petersen, *Die Drei*, 2002:4, p. 57. Of course, this is different from "literature" in the normal sense. Spiritual scientific descriptions, in the sense of Rudolf Steiner, need to be clothed differently than lyrical expression, for example, that have another origin.

121 Lecture of May 5, 1918, in GA 271, p. 138.

122 Lecture of May 6, 1918, in GA 271, p. 156.

123 Lecture of June 1, 1918, in GA 271, p. 183.

124 Ibid., p. 156.

125 Lecture of October 25, 1914, in GA 287, p. 73f.

126 Ibid.

127 Conversation with the dead is another aspect of the necessity for developing a new language that can be briefly mentioned here. Language, used purely in relation to ideas, is not perceptible to the dead. The inspiration brought to the living by the dead can also not take place. On the other hand, language we have felt our way into, language that uses the stylistic means presented in the previous chapters, can be "understood" by the dead.

128 Cf. Heinz Zimmermann, *Vom Sprachverlust zur neuen Bilderwelt des Wortes* [From the loss of language to a new imaginative world of the word] (Dornach, 2000), Chapter III; and *Grammatik. Spiel von Bewegung und Form* [Grammar: Play of movement and form] (Dornach, 1997), Chapter VII. Also Almut Bockemühl, „Märchen im Leben Rudolf Steiners," [Fairytales in the life of Rudolf Steiner], in *Das Goetheanum*, 45:1993, p. 475f.

CITED WORKS BY RUDOLF STEINER

GA 8   Das Christentum als mystische Tatsache und die
           Mysterien des Altertums, 9. Aufl. 1989
GA 11   Aus der Akasha-Chronik, 6. Aufl. 1986
GA 13   Die Geheimwissenschaft im Umriß, 30. Aufl. 1989
GA 14   Vier Mysteriendramen, 5. Aufl. 1998
GA 18   Die Rätsel der Philosophie, 9. Aufl. 1985
GA 20   Vom Menschenrätsel, 5. Aufl. 1984
GA 28   Mein Lebensgang, 9. Aufl. 2000
GA 35   Philosophie und Anthroposophie, 2. Aufl. 1984
GA 36   Der Goetheanumgedanke inmitten der Kulturkri-
           sis der Gegenwart, 1. Aufl. 1961
GA 40   Wahrspruchworte, 8. Aufl. 1998
GA 45   Anthroposophie. Ein Fragment aus dem Jahre
           1910, 4. Aufl. 2002
GA 56   Die Erkenntnis der Seele und des Geistes, 2. Aufl.
           1985
GA 59   Metamorphosen des Seelenlebens/ Pfade der See-
           lenerlebnisse, II, 1. Aufl. 1984
GA 64   Aus schicksaltragender Zeit, 1. Aufl. 1959
GA 83   Westliche und Östliche Weltgegensätzlichkeit,
           3.erg. Aufl. 1981
GA 84   Was wollte das Goetheanum und was soll die An-
           throposophie?, 2. Aufl. 1986
GA 122   Die Geheimnisse der biblischen Schöpfungsge-
           schichte, 6. Aufl. 1984
GA 124   Exkurse in das Gebiet des Markus-Evangeliums, 4.,
           neu durchges. Aufl. 1995
GA 127   Die Mission der neuen Geistesoffenbarung, 2. Aufl.
           1989

GA 145   Welche Bedeutung hat die okkulte Entwickelung
          des Menschen für seine Hüllen – physischen Leib,
          Ätherleib, Astralleib – und sein Selbst?, 5. Aufl.
          1986
GA 159   Das Geheimnis des Todes, 2. Aufl. 1980
GA 161   Wege der geistigen Erkenntnis und der Erneue-
          rung künstlerischer Weltanschauung, 2. Aufl. 1999
GA 164   Der Wert des Denkens für eine den Menschen be-
          friedigende Erkenntnis, 1. Aufl. 1984
GA 174   Zeitgeschichtliche Betrachtungen. Das Karma der
          Unwahrhaftigkeit II, 2. Aufl. 1983
GA 176   Menschliche und menschheitliche Entwicklungs-
          wahrheiten. Das Karma des Materialismus, 2. Aufl.
          1982
GA 190   Vergangenheits- und Zukunftsimpulse im sozialen
          Geschehen, 3. Aufl. 1980
GA 196   Geistige und soziale Wandlungen in der Mensch-
          heitsentwickelung, 2. Aufl. 1992
GA 203   Die Verantwortung des Menschen für die Weltent-
          wickelung, 2. Aufl. 1989
GA 215   Die Philosophie, Kosmologie und Religion in der
          Anthroposophie, 2. Aufl. 1980
GA 217   Geistige Wirkenskräfte im Zusammenleben von al-
          ter und junger Generation, 6. Aufl. 1988
GA 253   Probleme des Zusammenlebens in der Anthroposo-
          phischen Gesellschaft. Zur Dornacher Krise vom
          Jahre 1915, 1. Aufl. 1989
GA 258   Die Geschichte und die Bedingungen der anthro-
          posophischen Bewegung im Verhältnis zur Anthro-
          posophischen Gesellschaft, 3. Aufl. 1981
GA 259   Das Schicksalsjahr 1923 in der Geschichte der An-
          throposophischen Gesellschaft, 1. Aufl. 1991
GA 266/1 Aus den Inhalten der esoterischen Stunden I, 1.
          Aufl. 1995
GA 266/3 Aus den Inhalten der esoterischen Stunden III, 1.
          Aufl. 1998
GA 271   Kunst und Kunsterkenntnis, 3., erw. Aufl. 1985

GA 277   Eurythmie – Die Offenbarung der sprechenden Seele, 3. Aufl. 1999

GA 277a   Die Entstehung und Entwickelung der Eurythmie, 3. Aufl. 1998

GA 279   Eurythmie als sichtbare Sprache, 5. Aufl. 1990

GA 280   Methodik und Wesen der Sprachgestaltung, 4. Aufl. 1983

GA 284   Bilder okkulter Siegel und Säulen, 3., erw. Aufl. 1993

GA 287   Der Dornacher Bau als Wahrzeichen geschichtlichen Werdens und künstlerischer Umwandlungsimpulse, 2. Aufl. 1985

GA 294   Erziehungskunst. Methodisch-Didaktisches, 6. Aufl. 1990

GA 297   Idee und Praxis der Waldorfschule, 1. Aufl. 1998

GA 299   Geisteswissenschaftliche Sprachbetrachtungen, 4. Aufl. 1981

GA 301   Die Erneuerung der pädagogisch-didaktischen Kunst durch Geisteswissenschaft, 4. Aufl. 1991

GA 311   Die Kunst des Erziehens aus dem Erfassen der Menschenwesenheit, 5. Aufl. 1989

GA 322   Grenzen der Naturerkenntnis und ihre Überwindung, 5. Aufl. 1981

GA 334   Vom Einheitsstaat zum dreigliedrigen sozialen Organismus, 1. Aufl. 1983

GA 338   Wie wirkt man für den Impuls der Dreigliederung des sozialen Organismus?, 4., erw Aufl. 1986

GA 339   Anthroposophie, soziale Dreigliederung und Redekunst, 3. Aufl. 1984

GA 343   Vorträge und Kurse über christlich-religiöses Wirken II, 1. Aufl. 1993

GA 349   Vom Leben des Menschen und der Erde. Über das Wesen des Christentums, 2. Aufl. 1980

GA 350   Rhythmen im Kosmos und im Menschenwesen. Wie kommt man zum Schauen der geistigen Welt?, 3. Aufl. 1991

THE AUTHOR

Martina Maria Sam was born in 1960 in Hornbach/Oden-wald, Germany. From 1979-81, she studied sociology and political science at the University of Heidelberg. Between 1981 and 1986, she attended the Institute for Waldorf Pedagogy, Witten-Annen where she studied eurythmy and pedagogy. From 1987 to 1992, she was active as a eurythmist on the Goetheanum stage while, at the same time, working for various publishers. From 1989-2000, she assisted in the publication of the Rudolf Steiner *Gesamtausgabe* [Rudolf Steiner's collected works]. During the same period, she studied art history, German, and history at the University of Basel where she wrote her Master's thesis on Rudolf Steiner's blackboard drawings (*Bildspuren der Imagination* [Image traces of imagination], Dornach, 2000). From 1996-98 she served as editor of the weekly newspaper, *Das Goetheanum*. In January, 2000, she assumed the leadership of the *Sektion für Schöne Wissenschaften* (Literary Arts and Humanities Section) of the School for Spiritual Science at the Goetheanum.